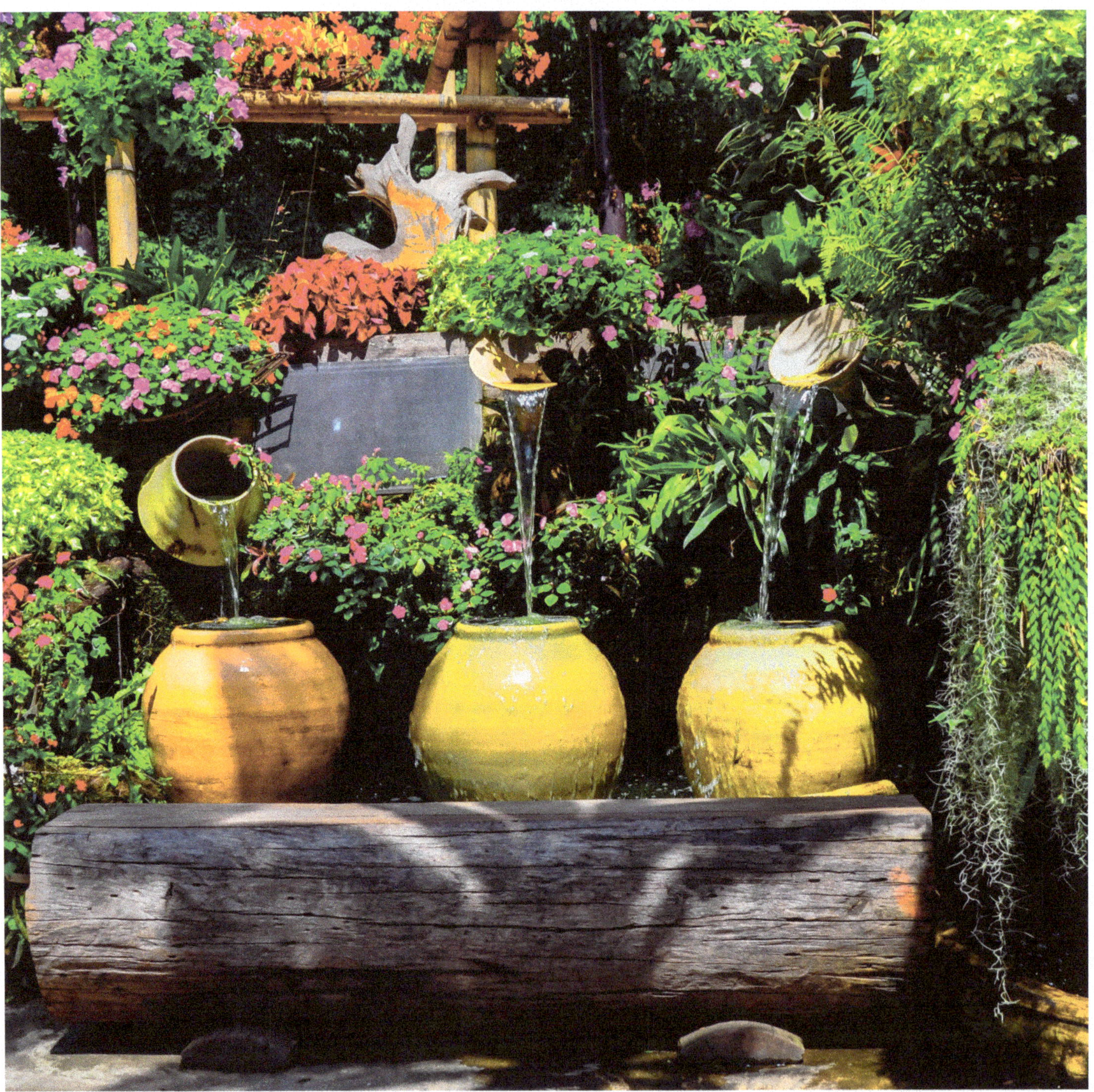

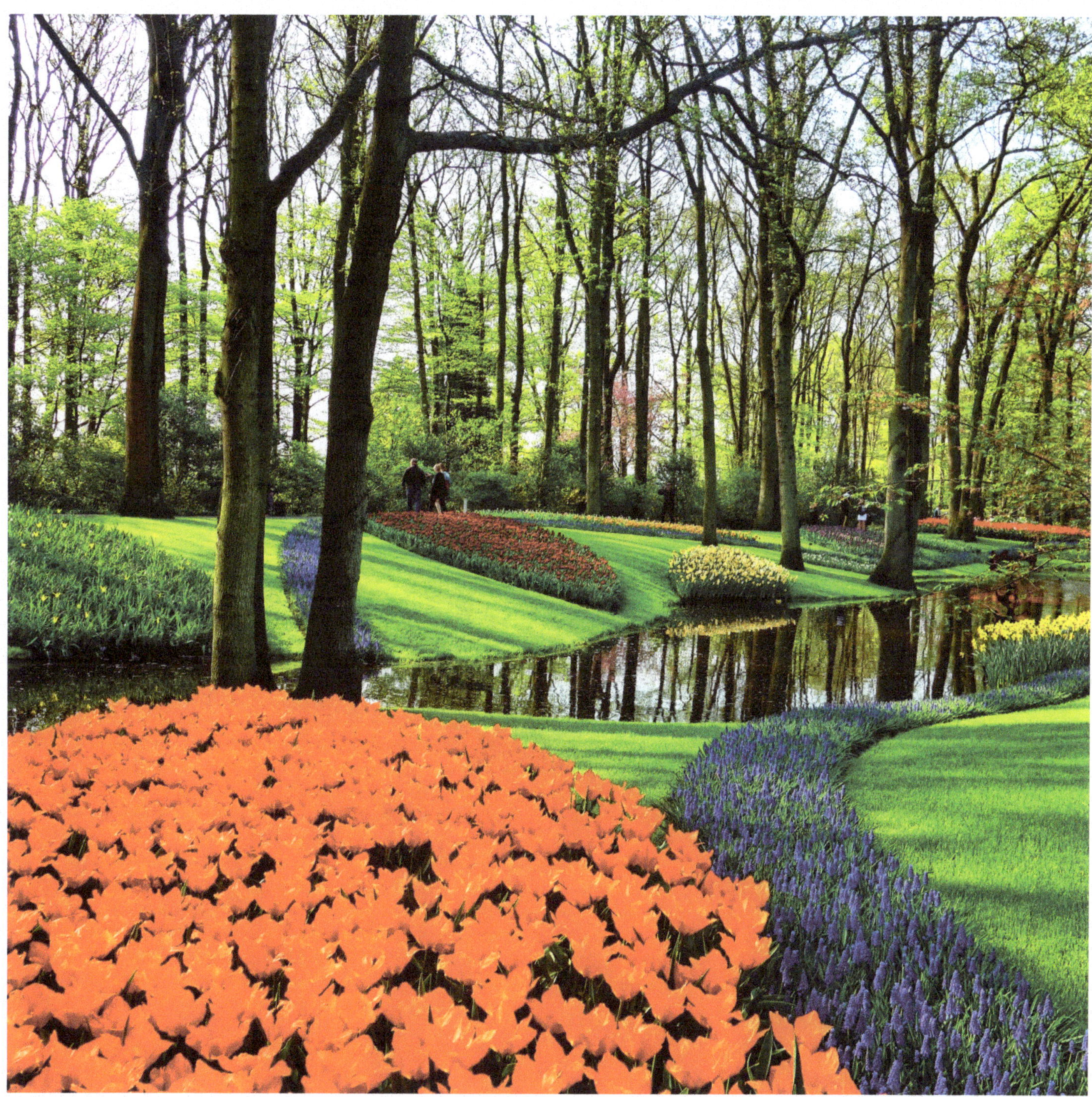

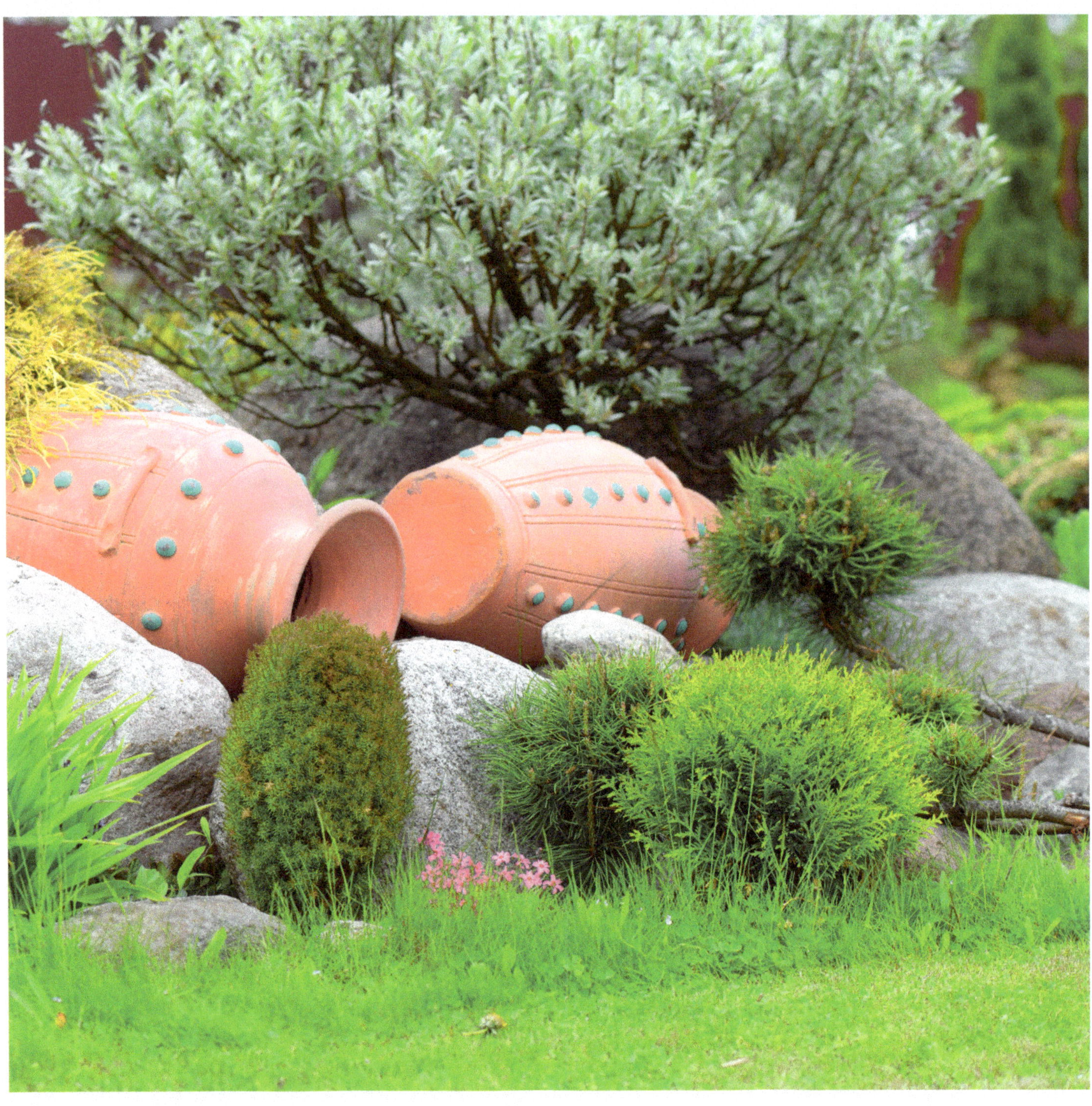

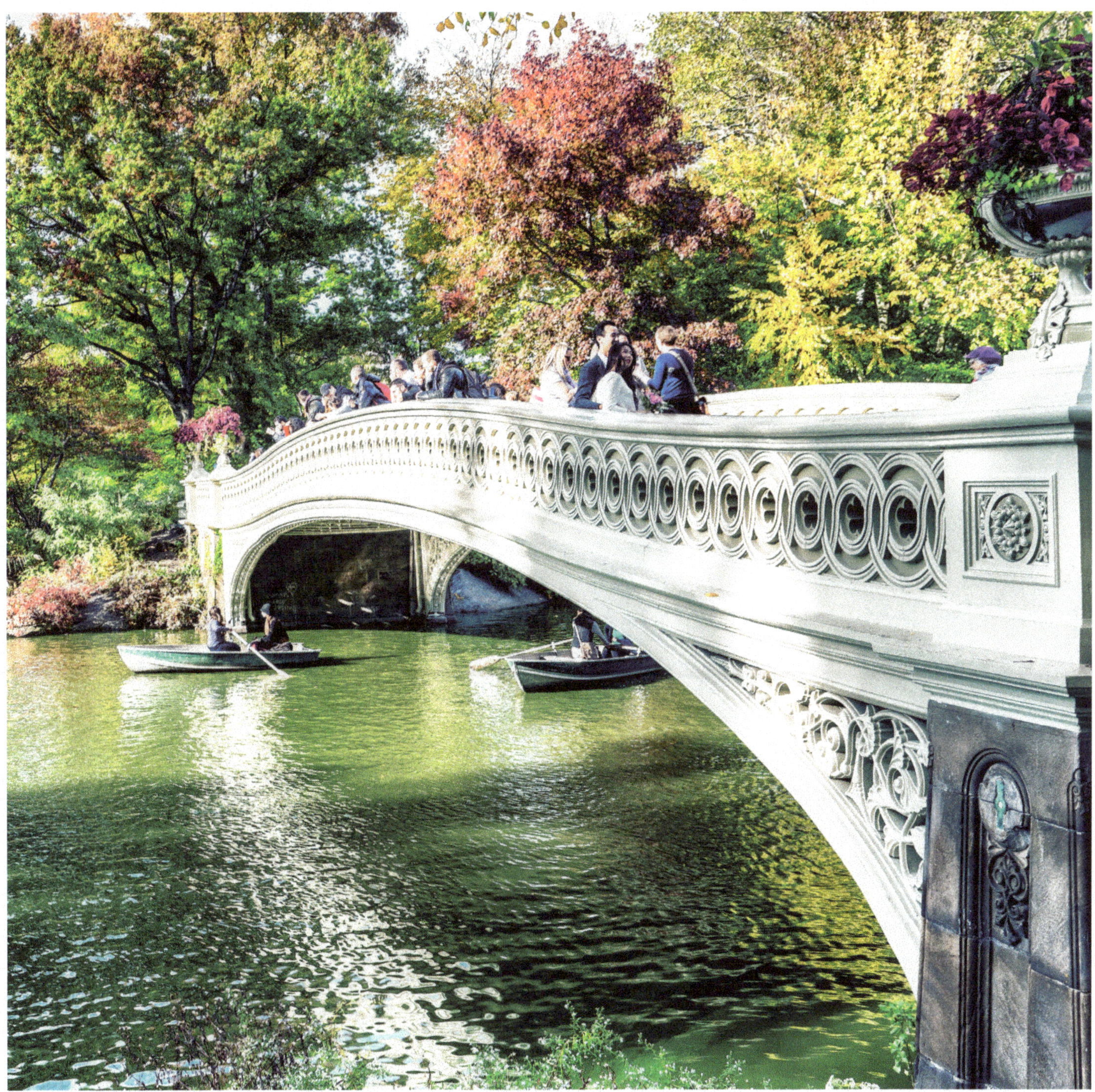

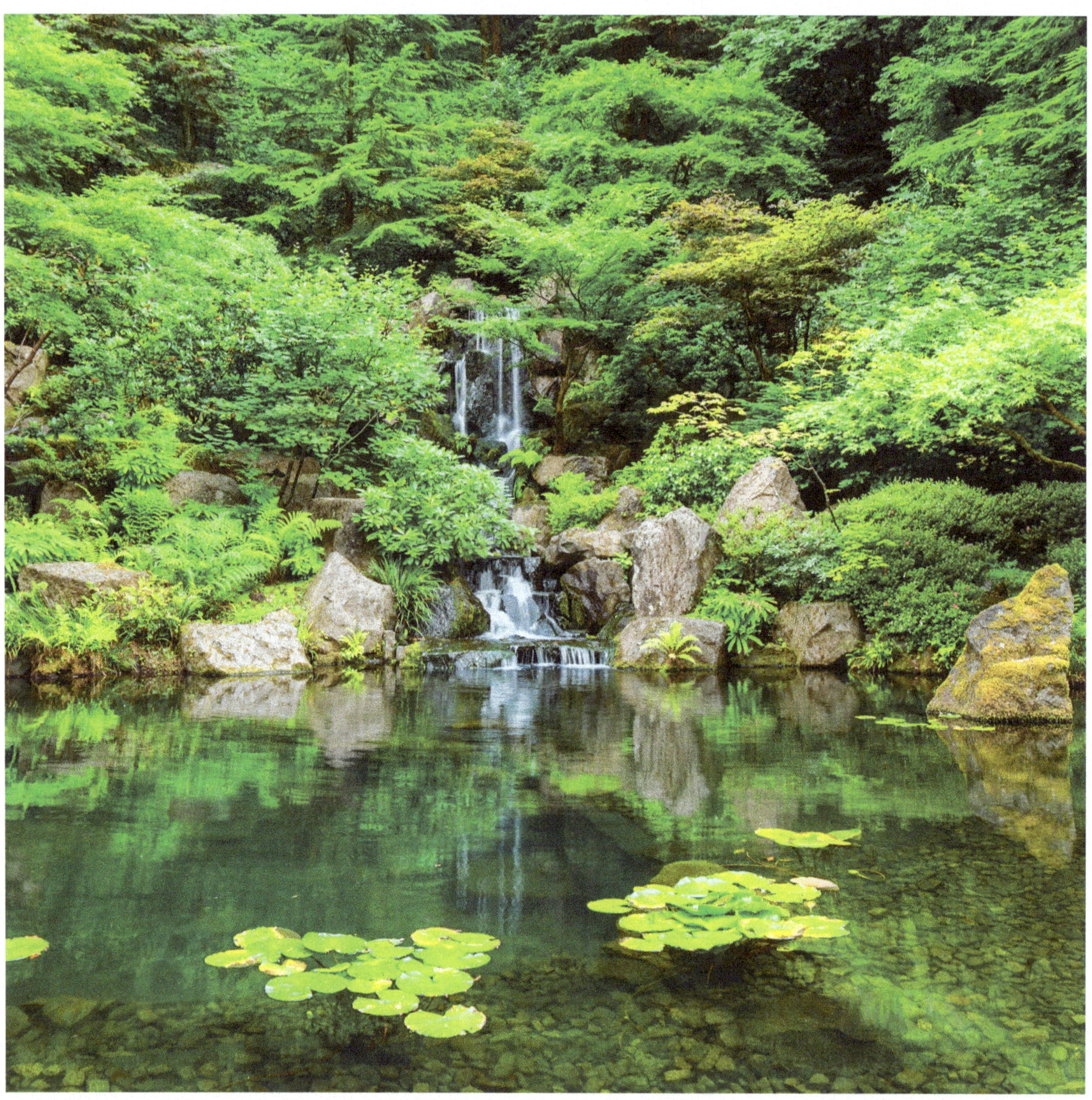

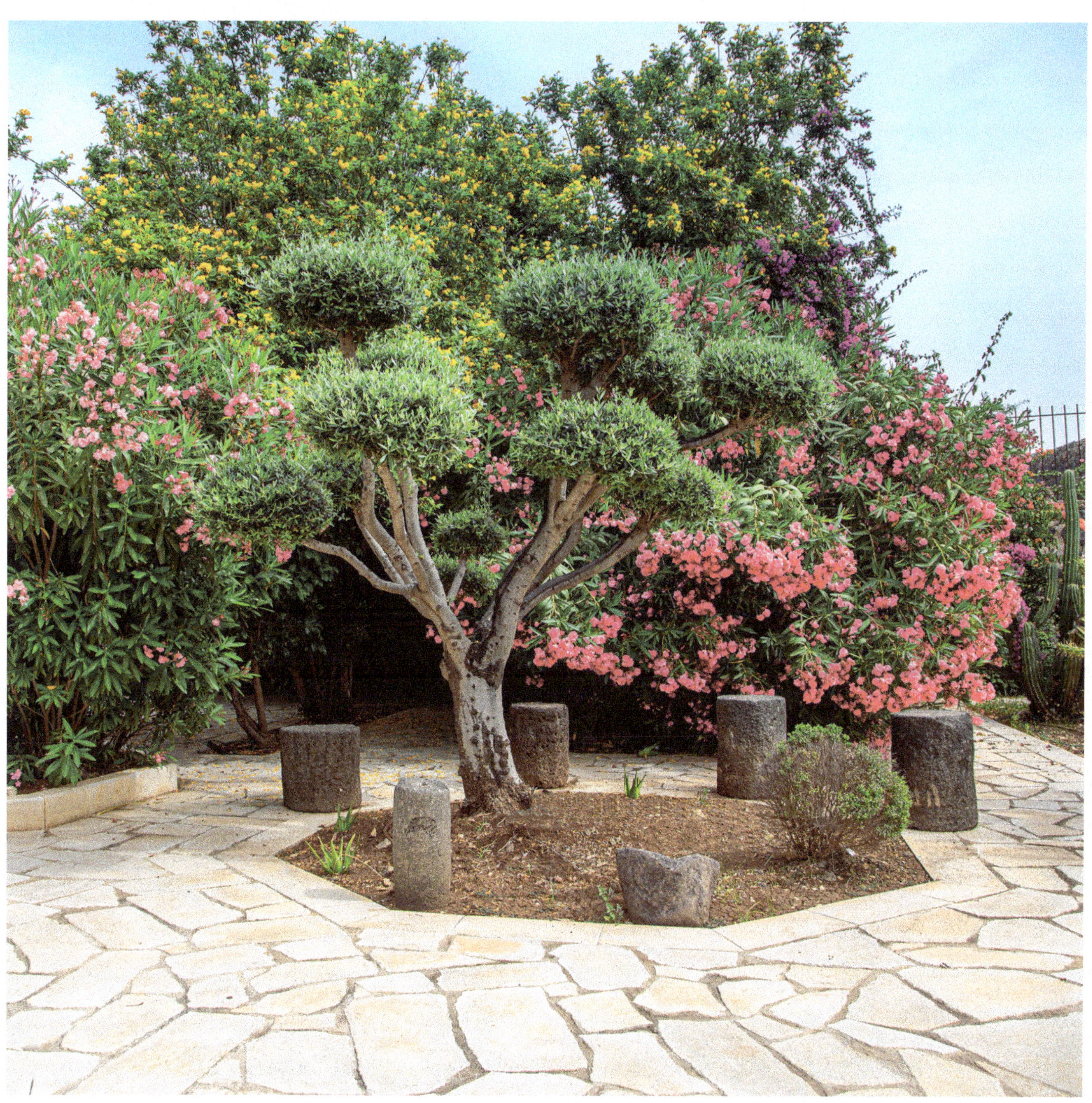

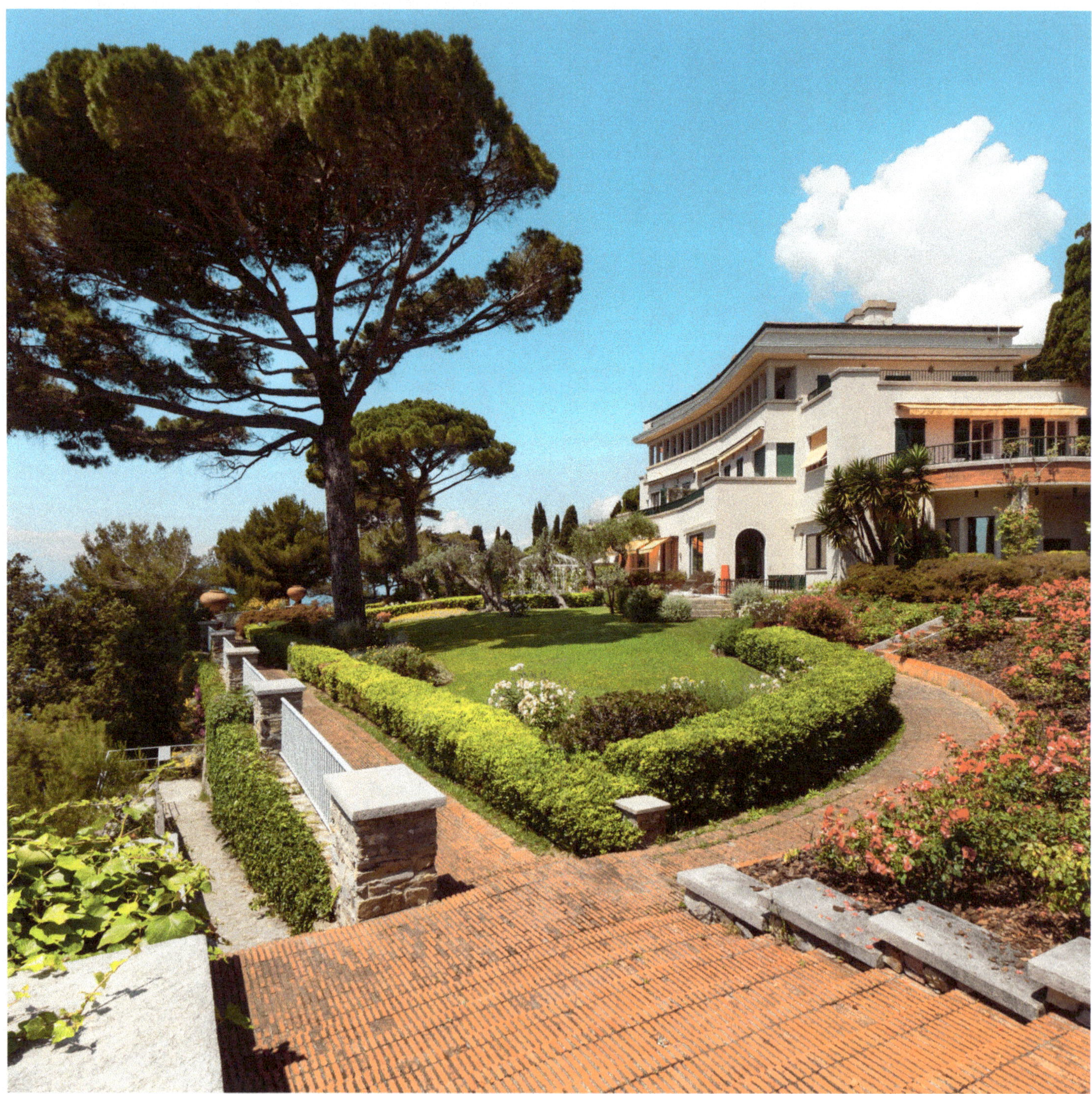

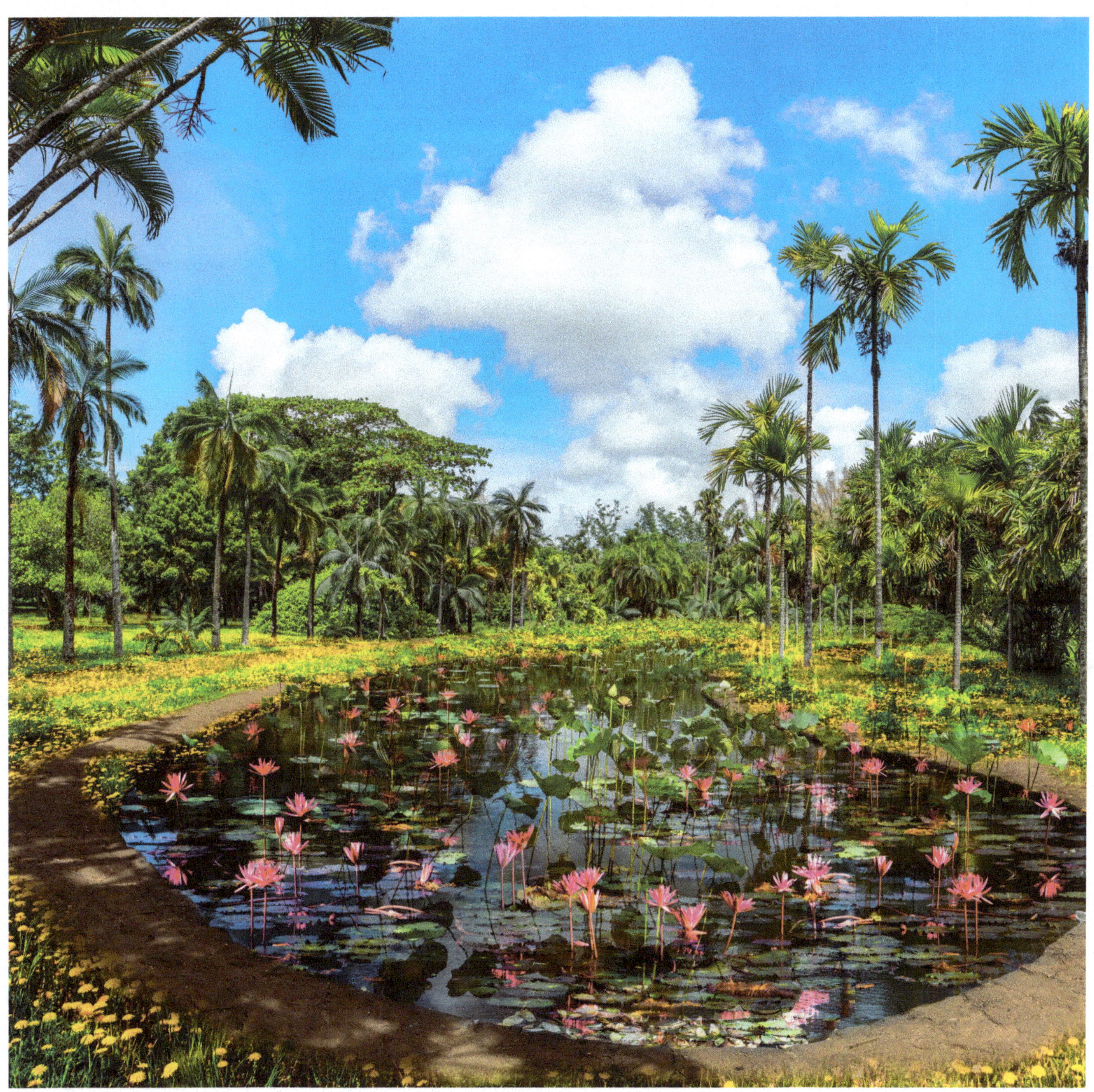

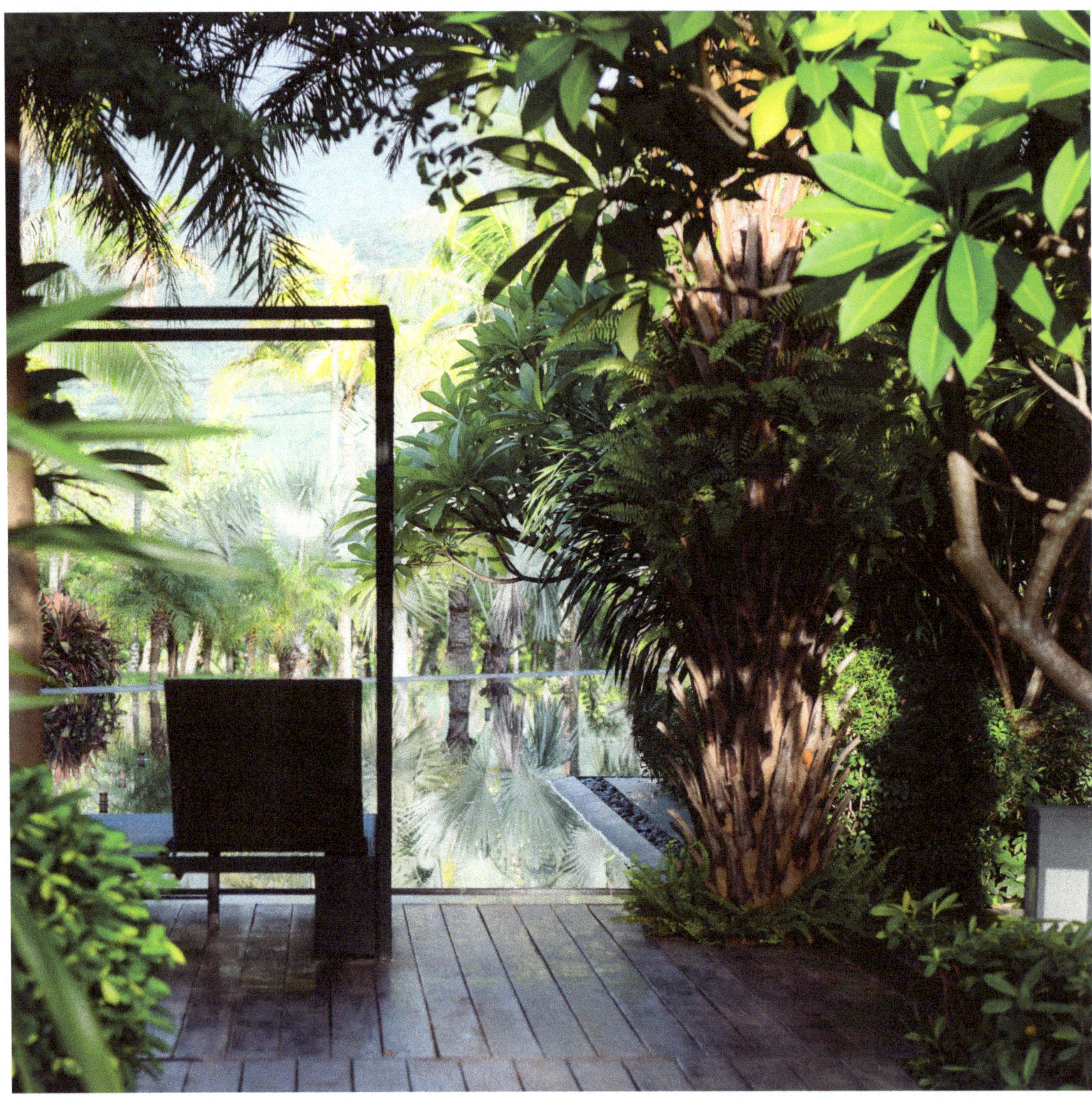

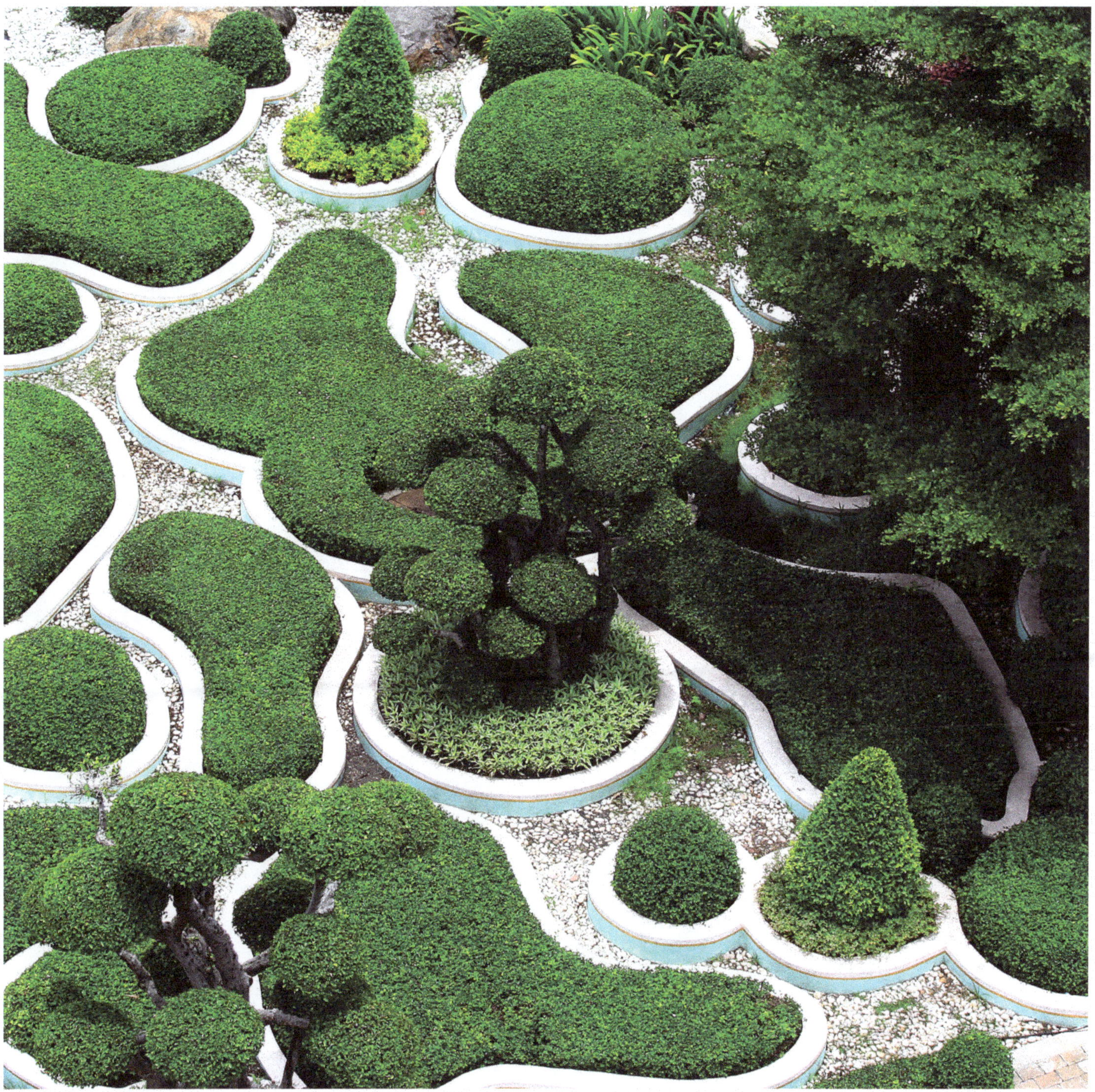

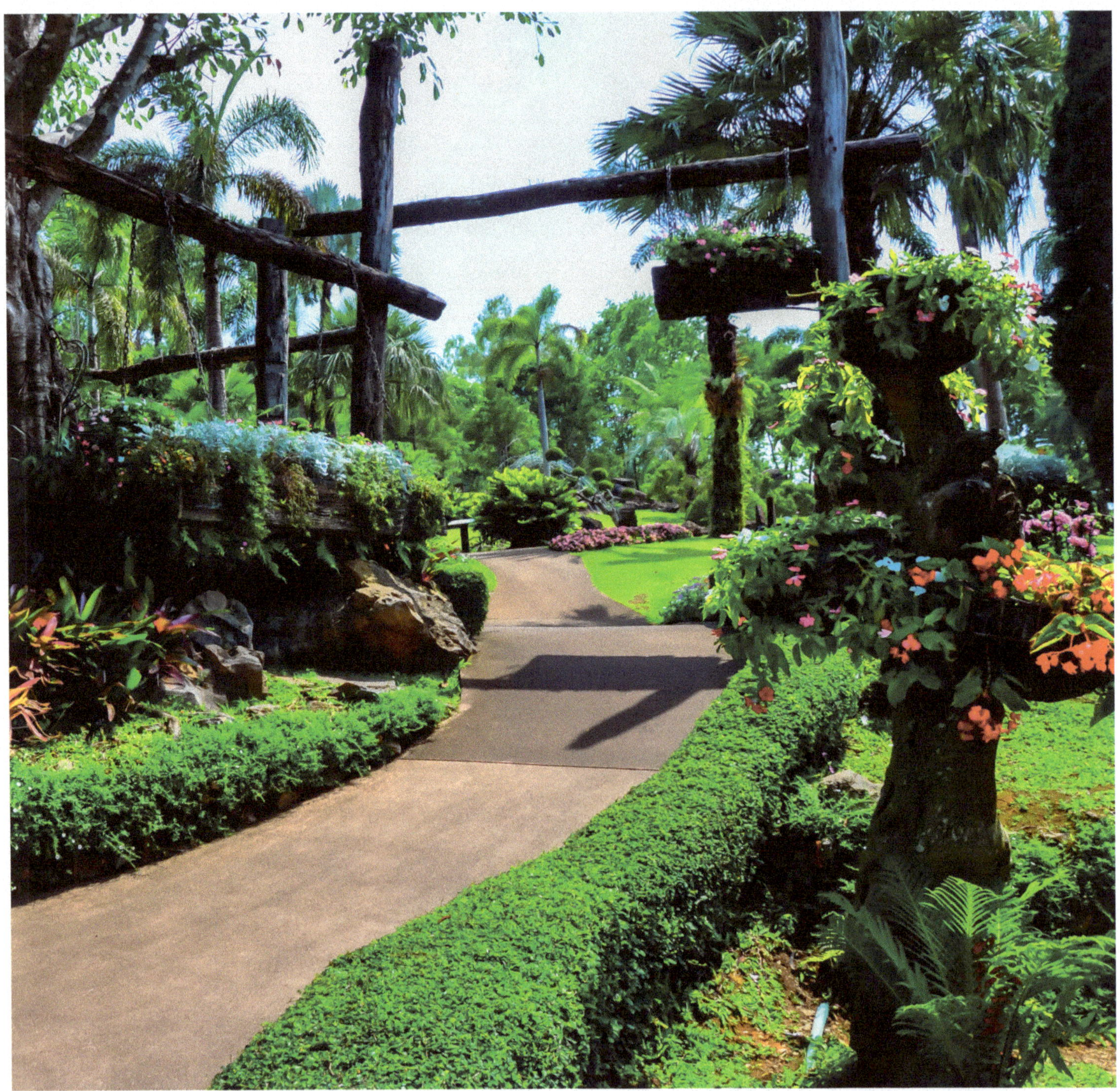

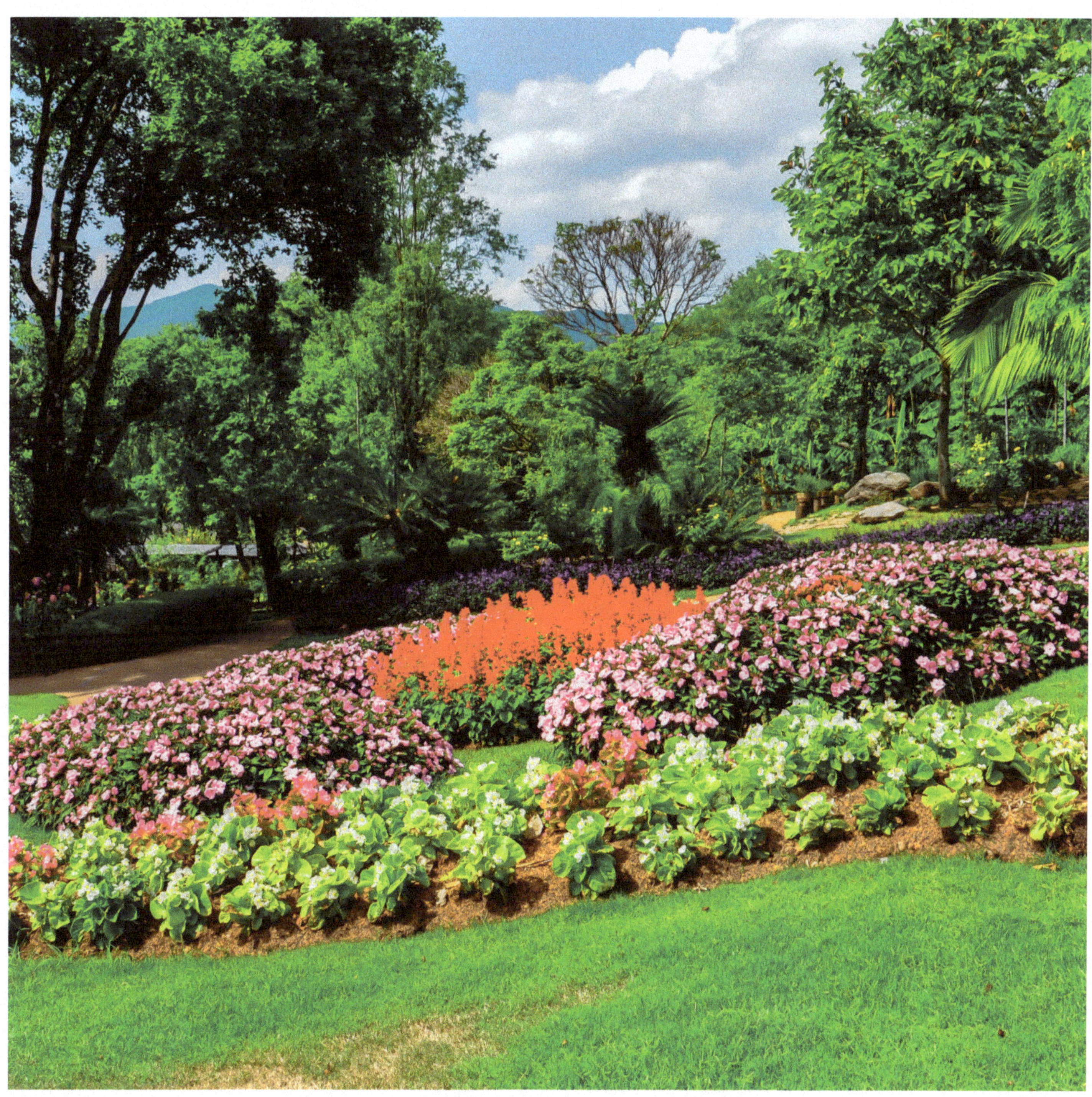

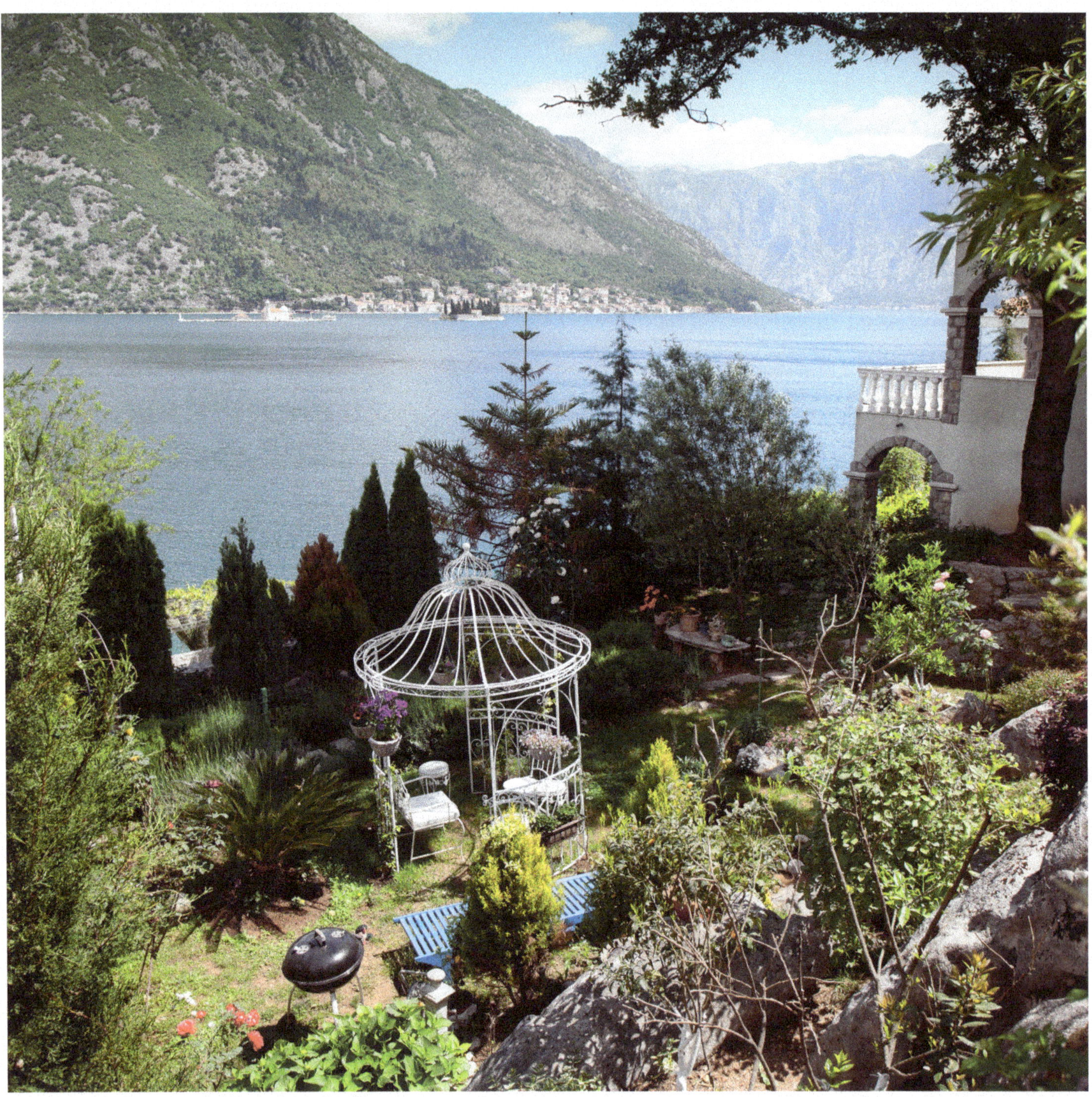

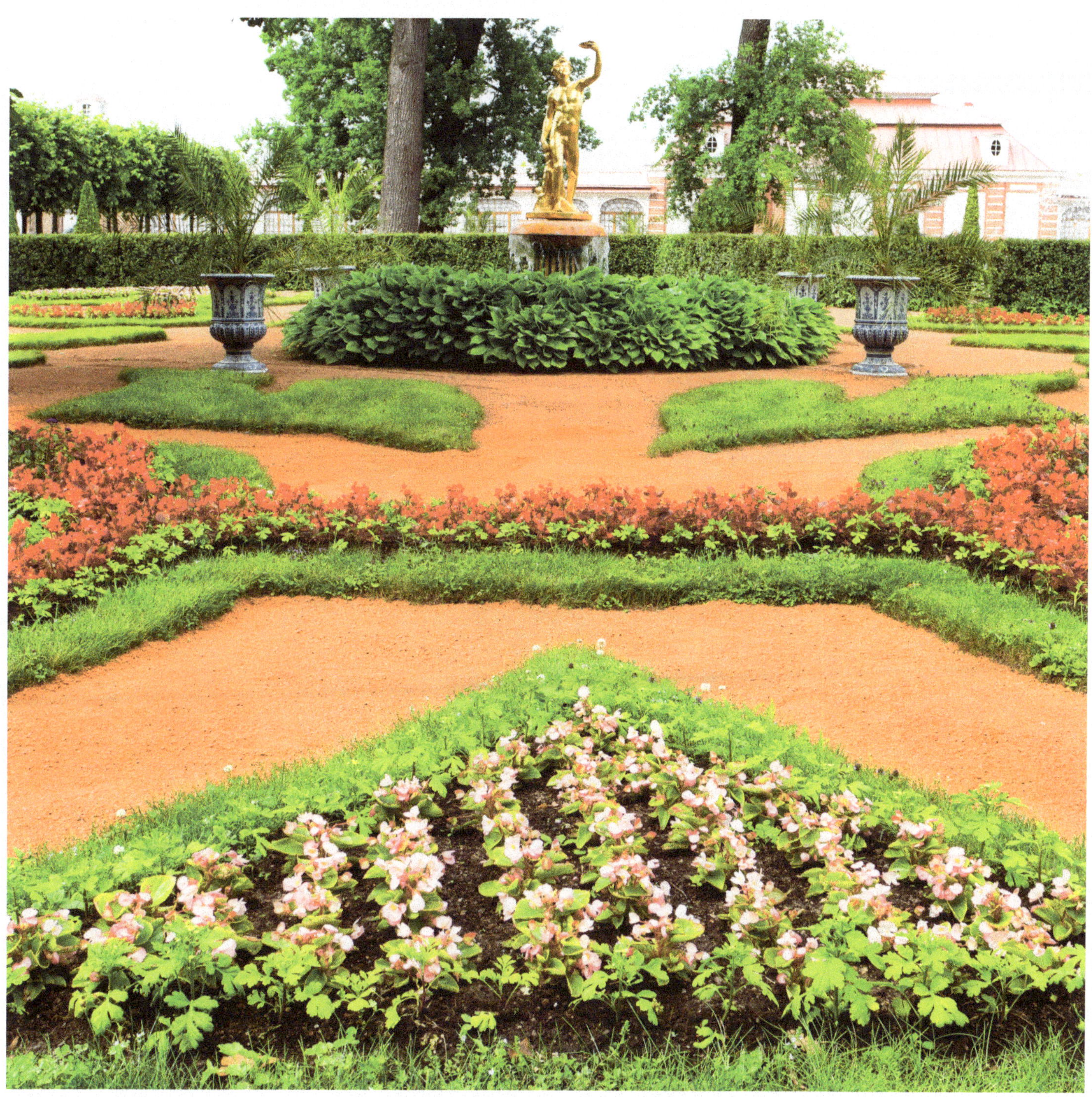

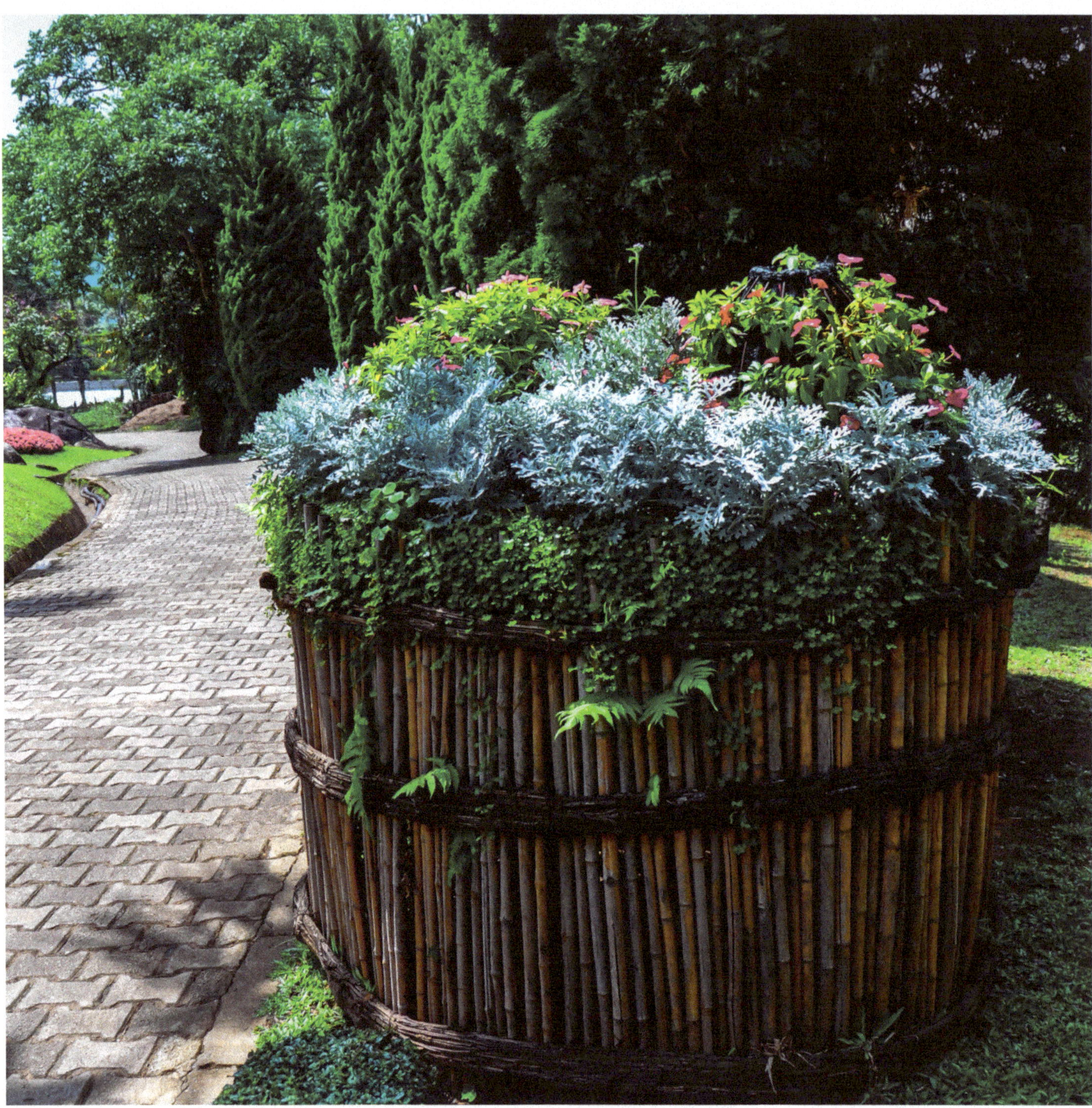

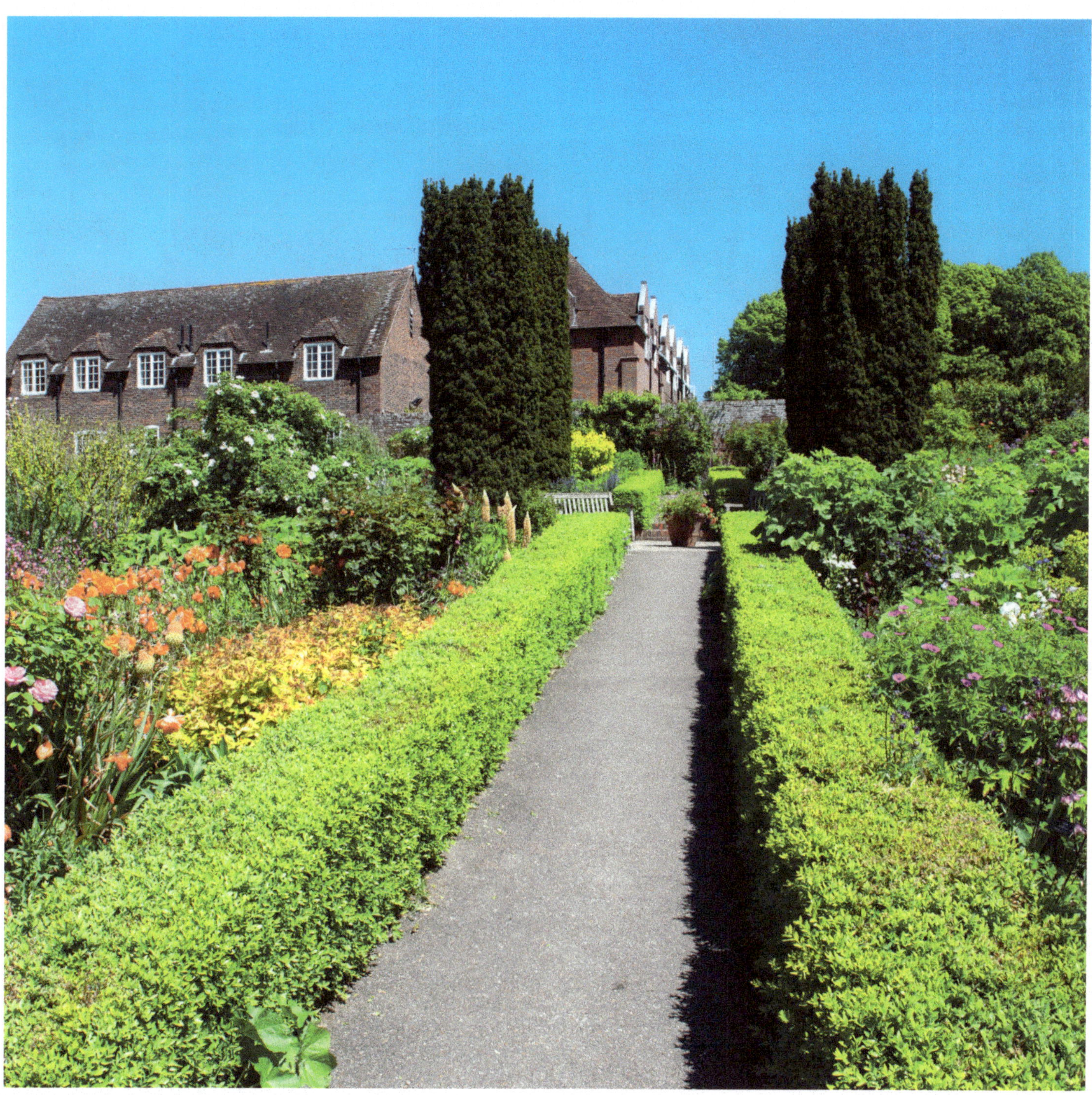

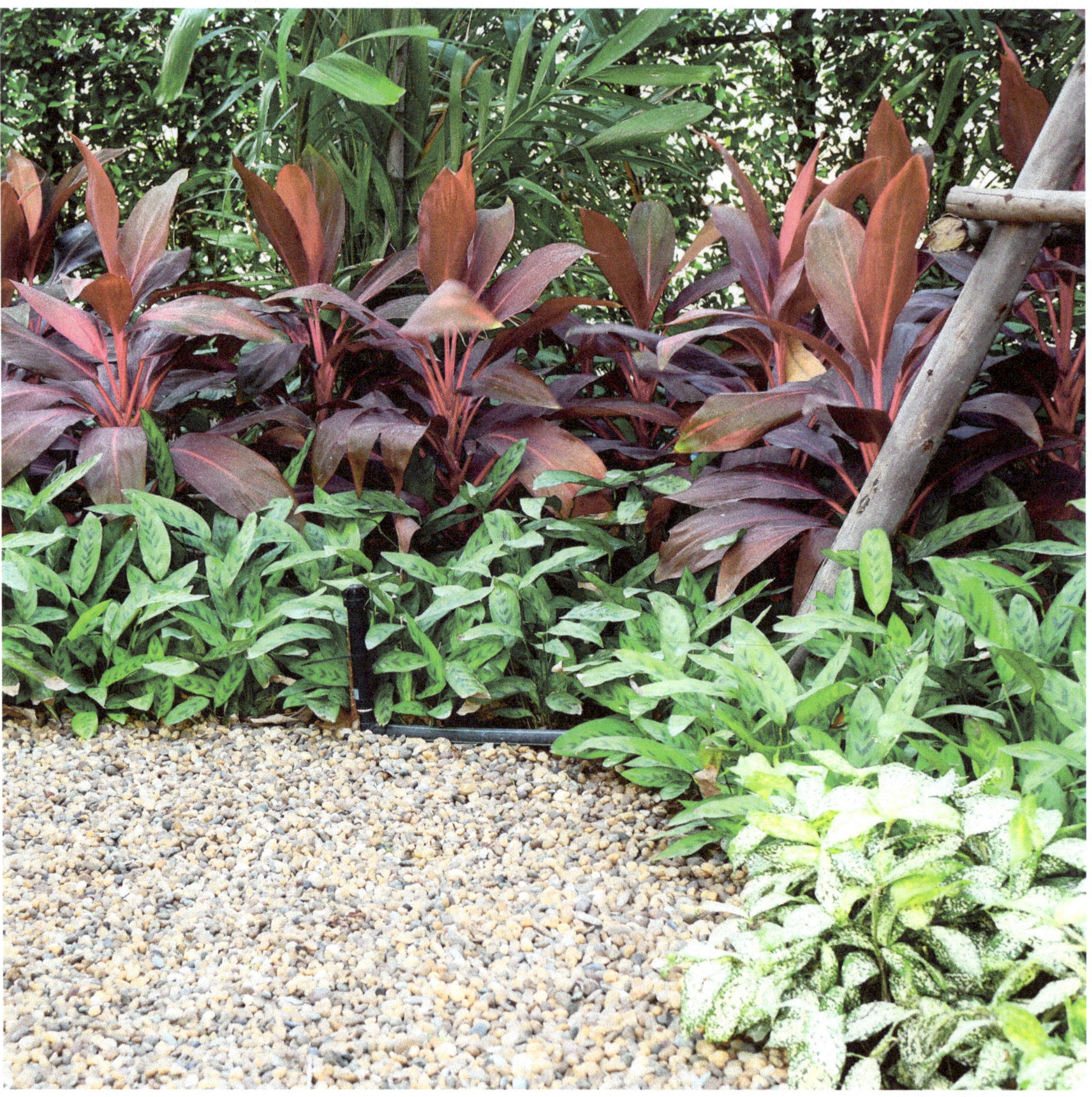

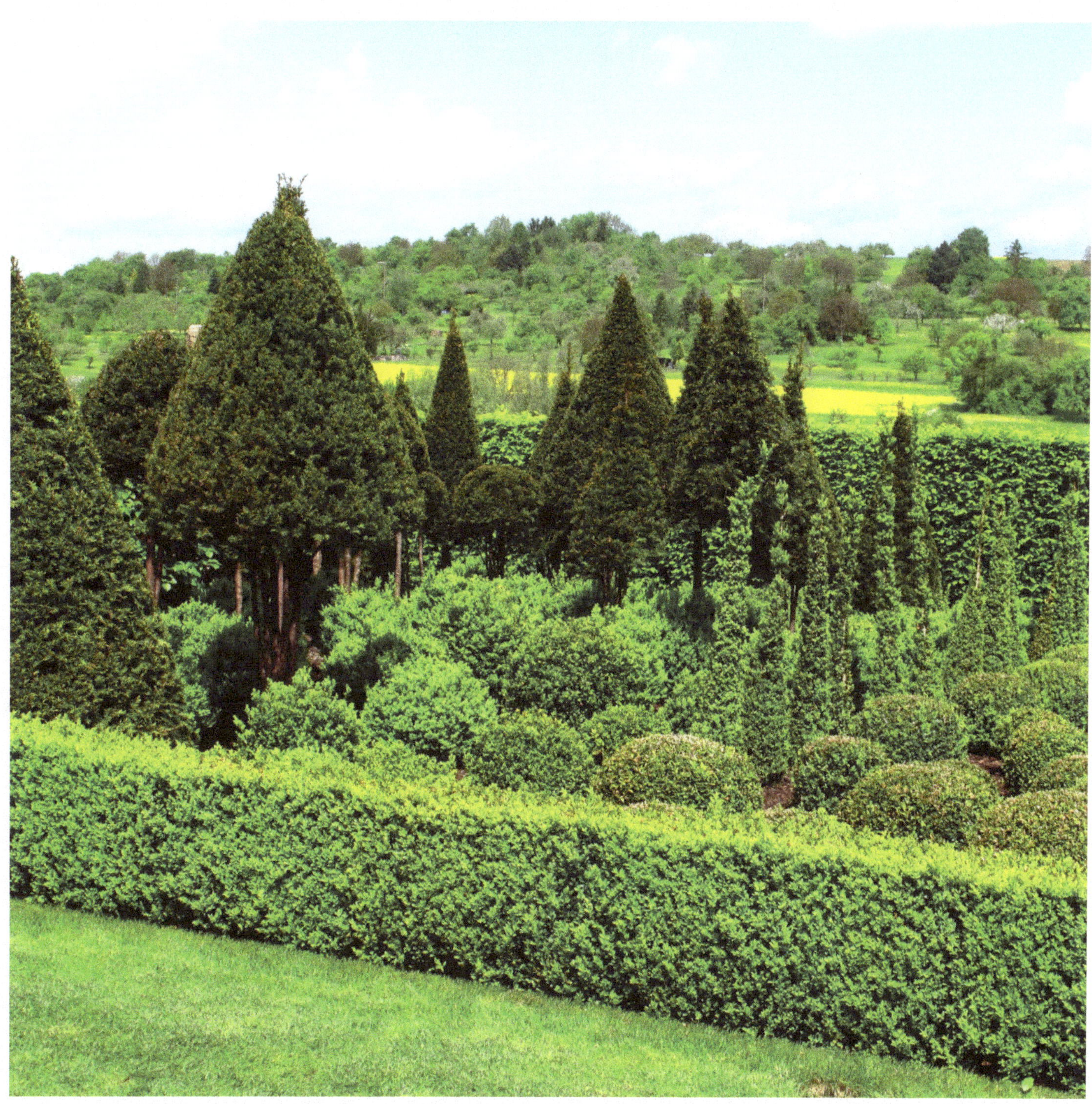

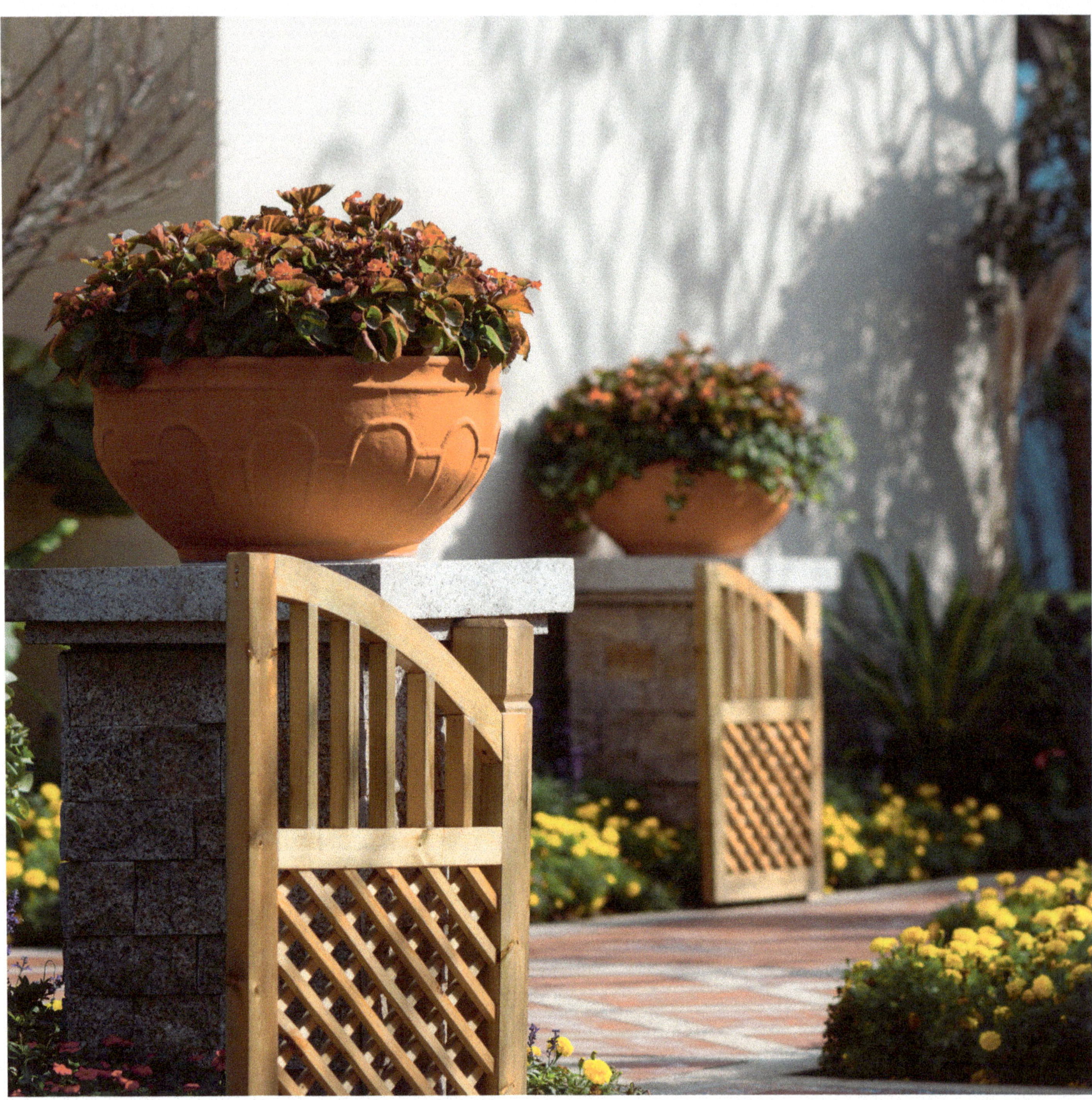

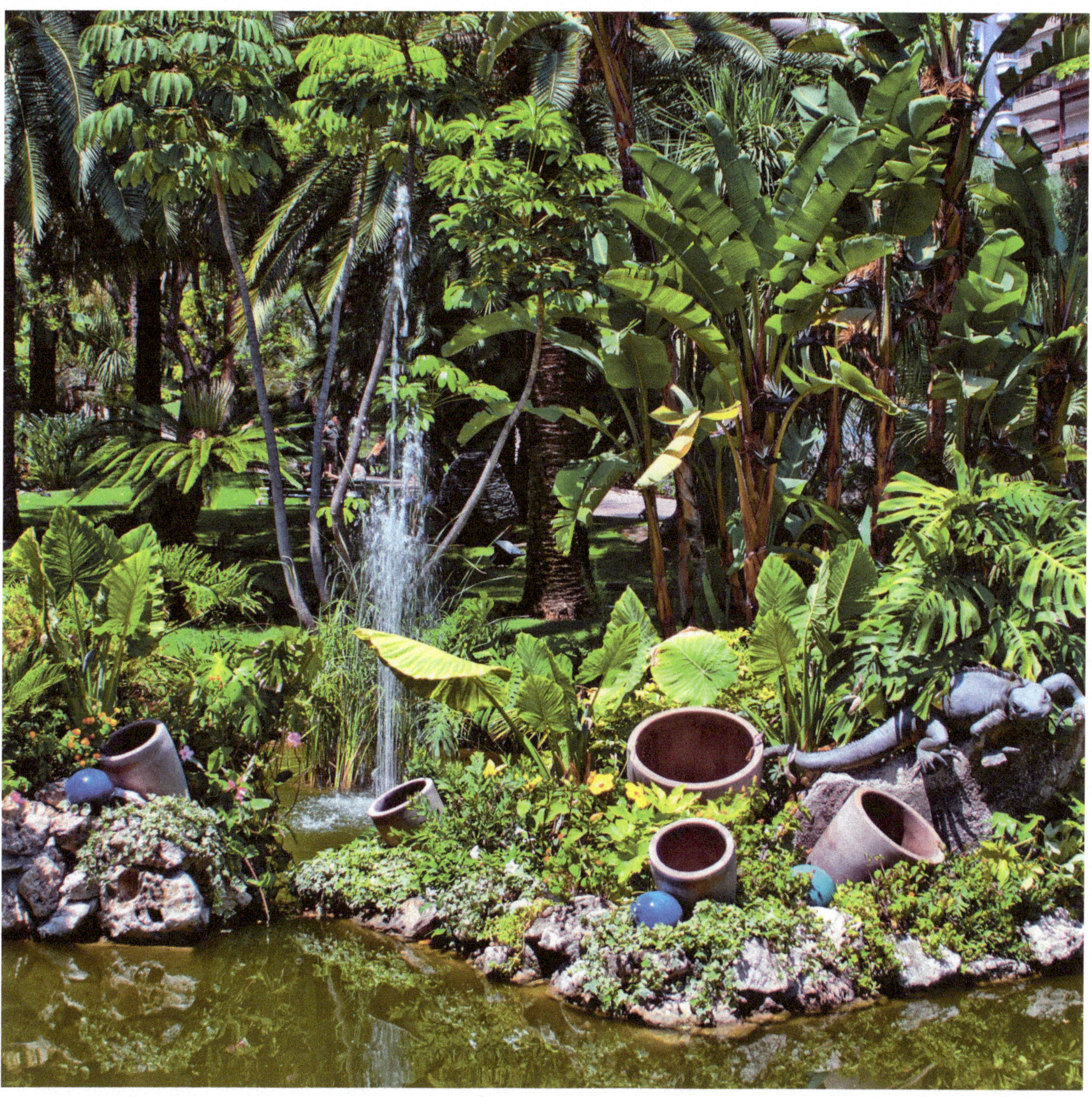

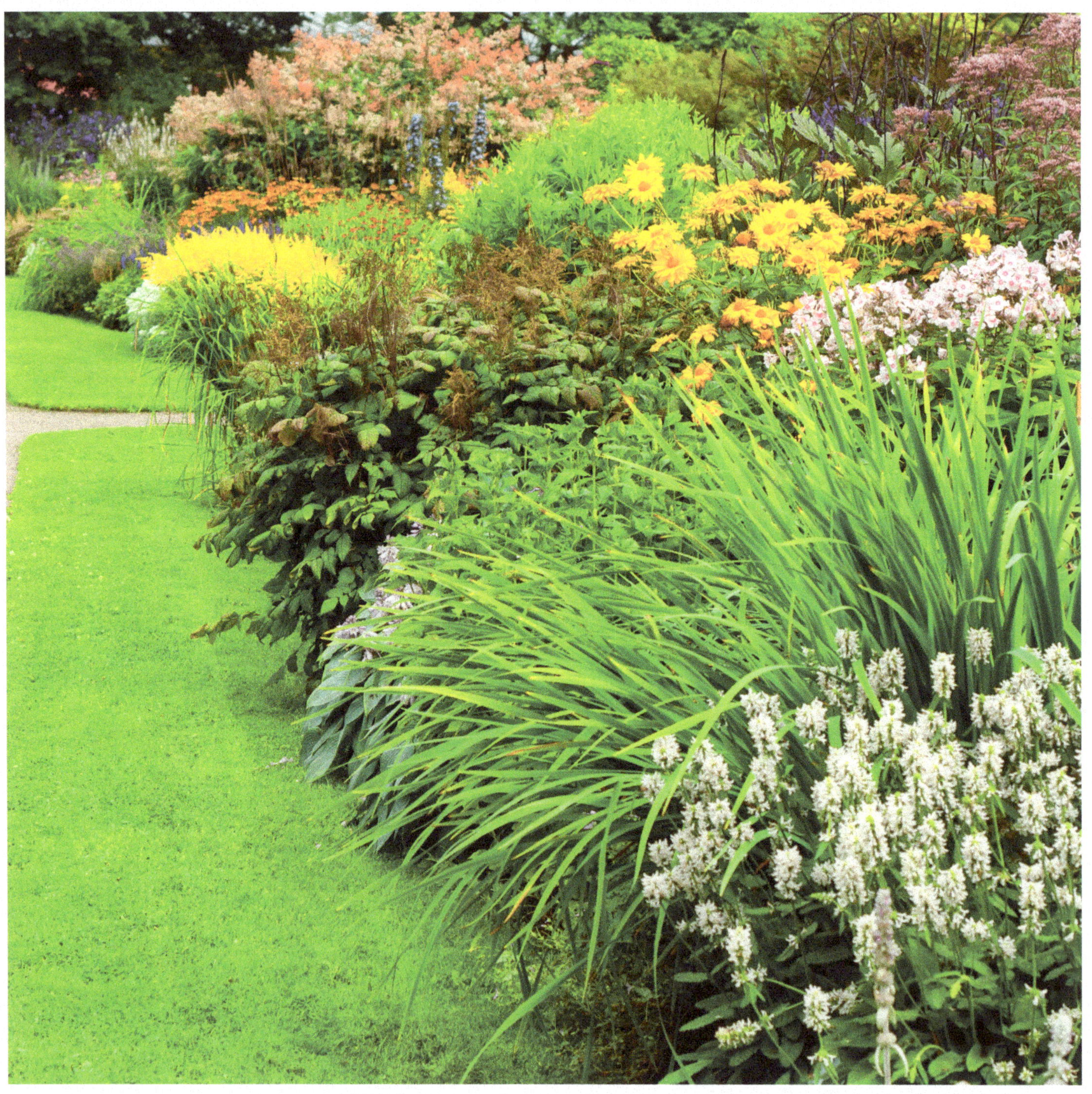

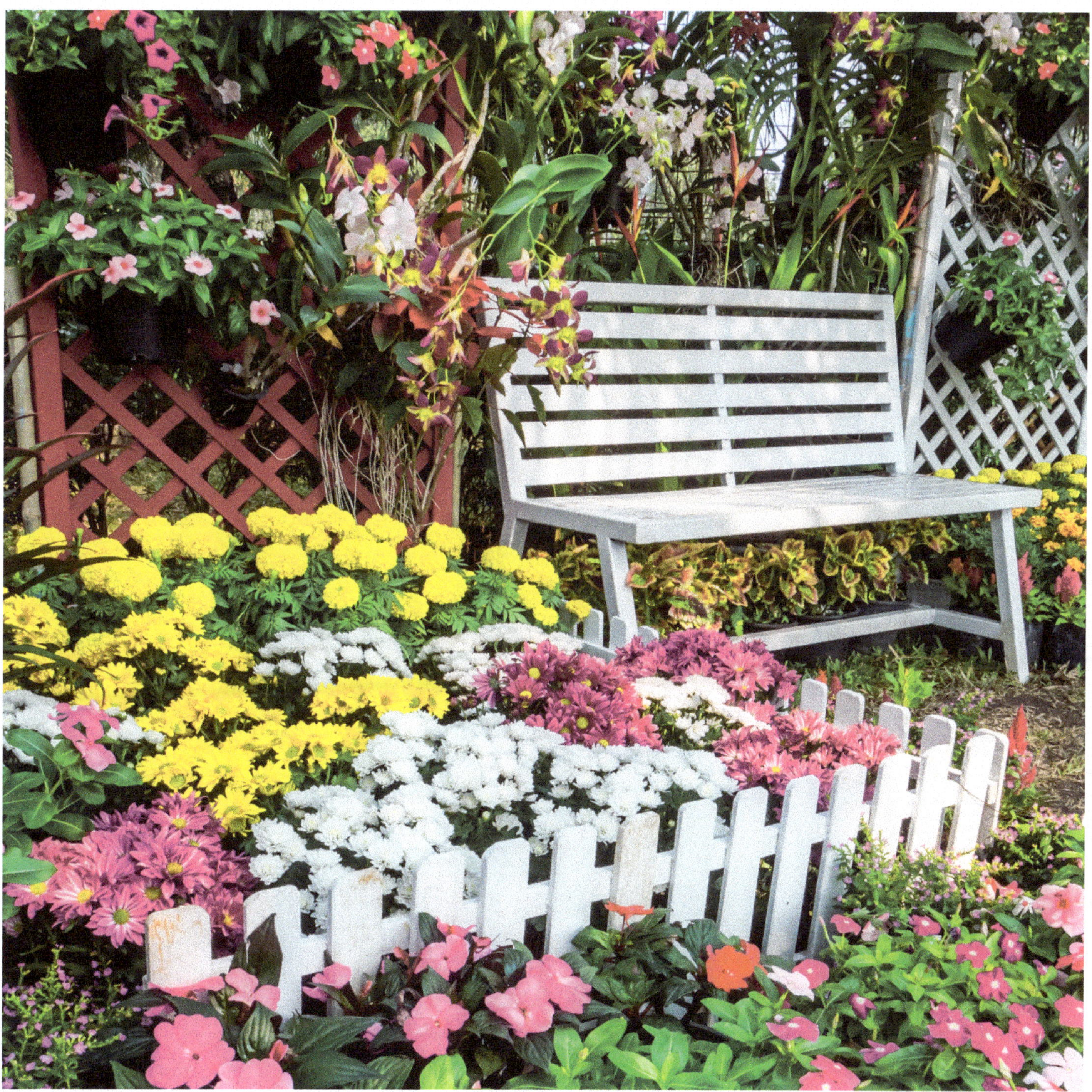

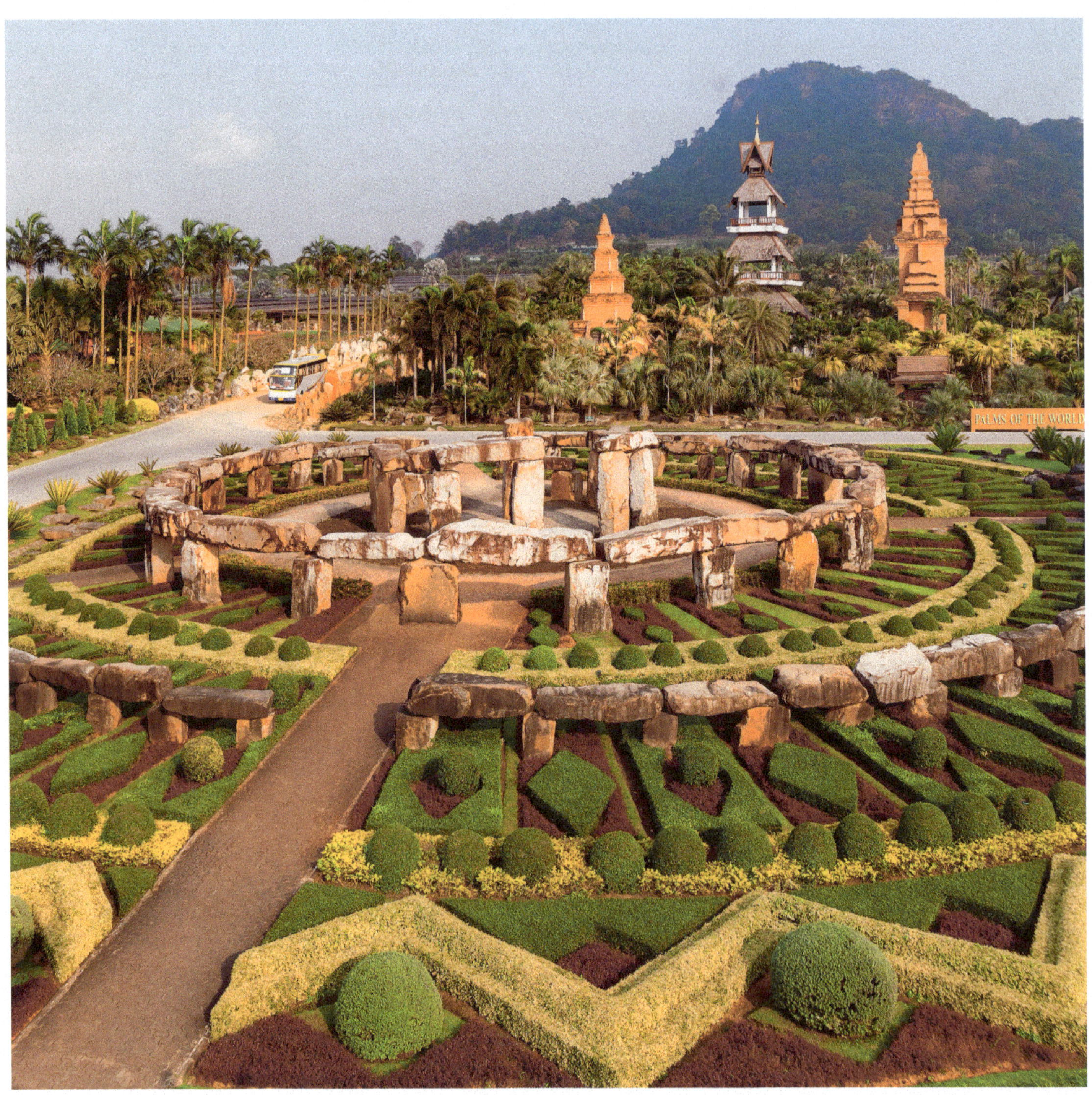
PALMS OF THE WORLD

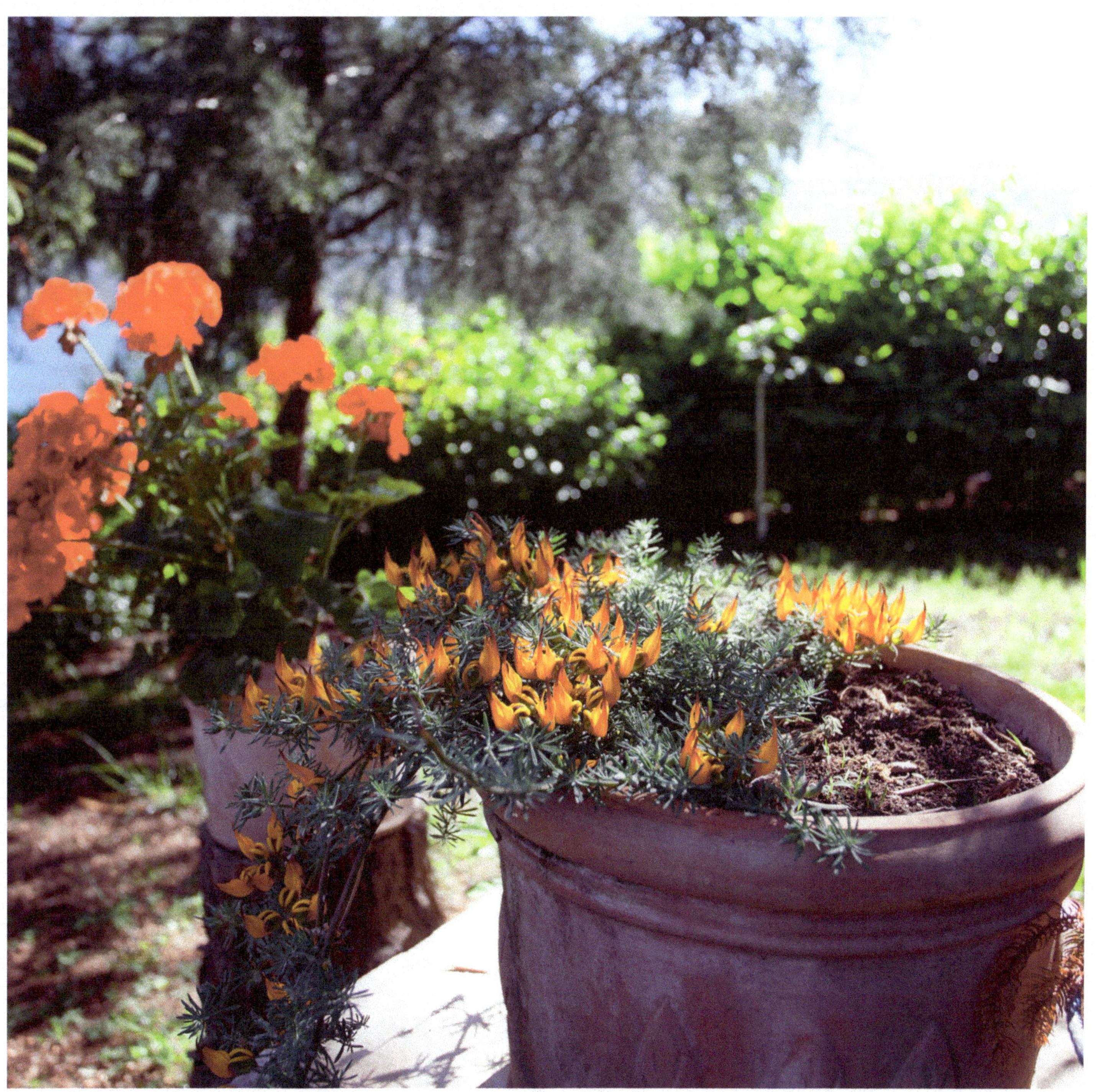

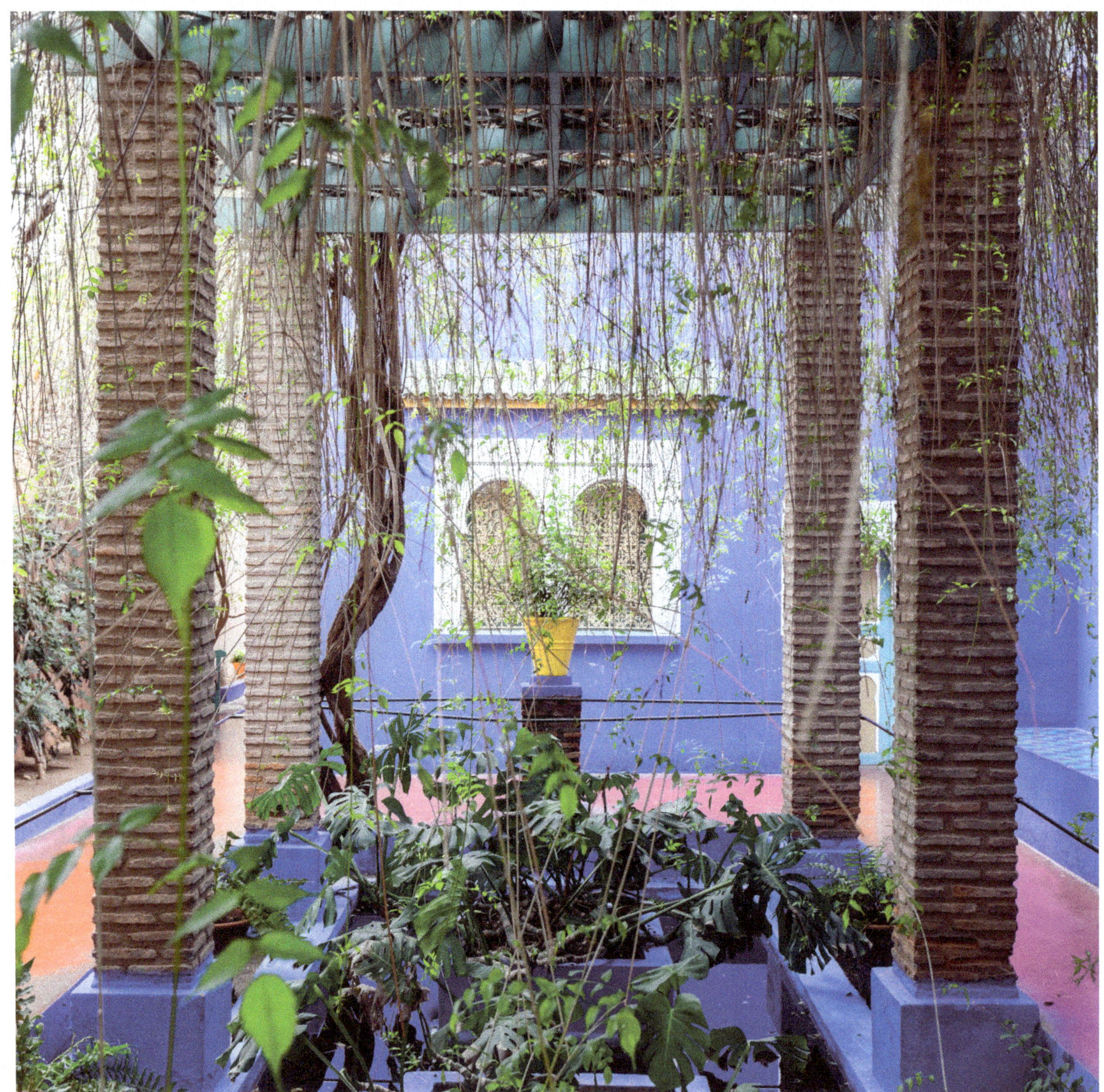

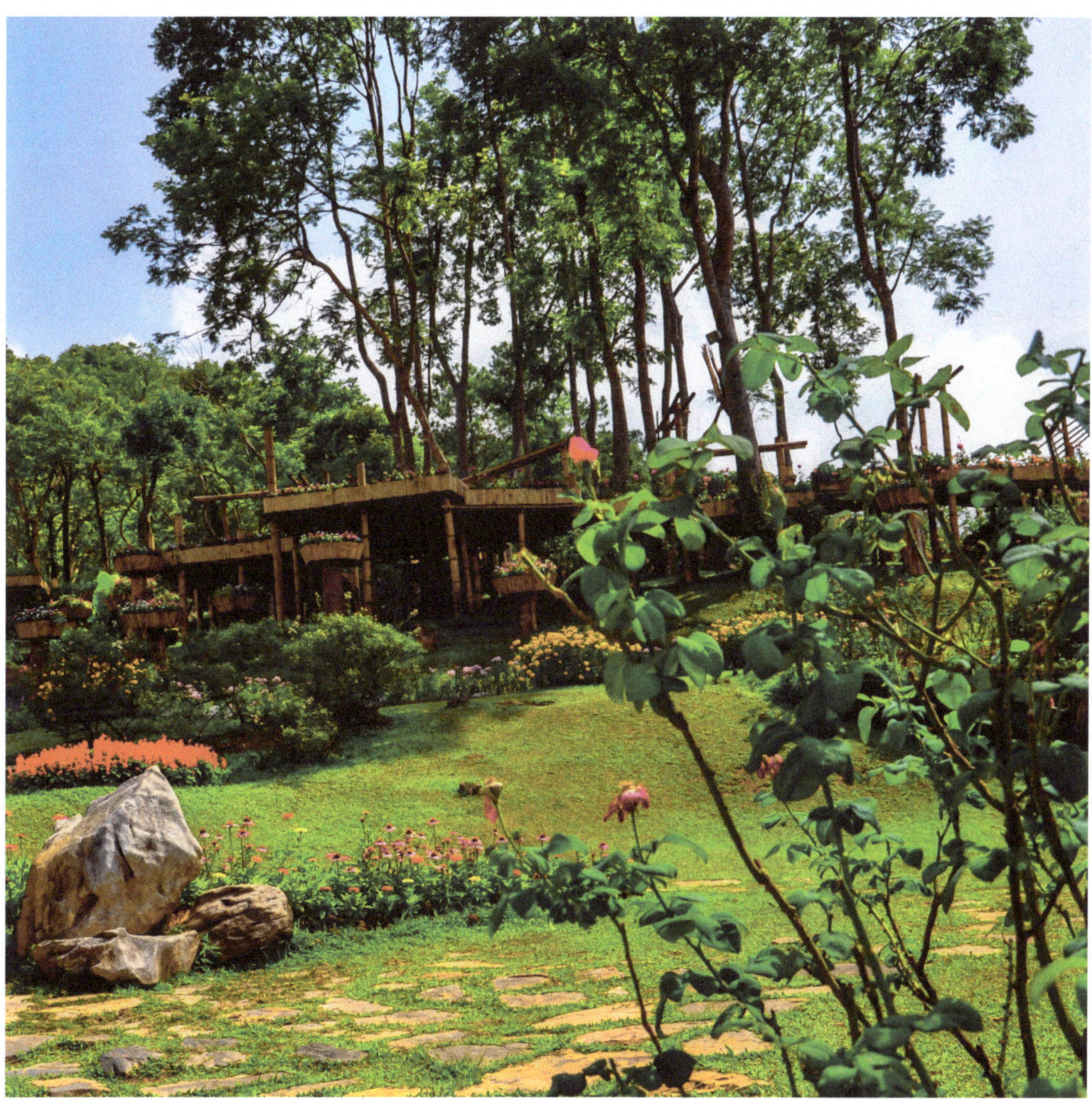

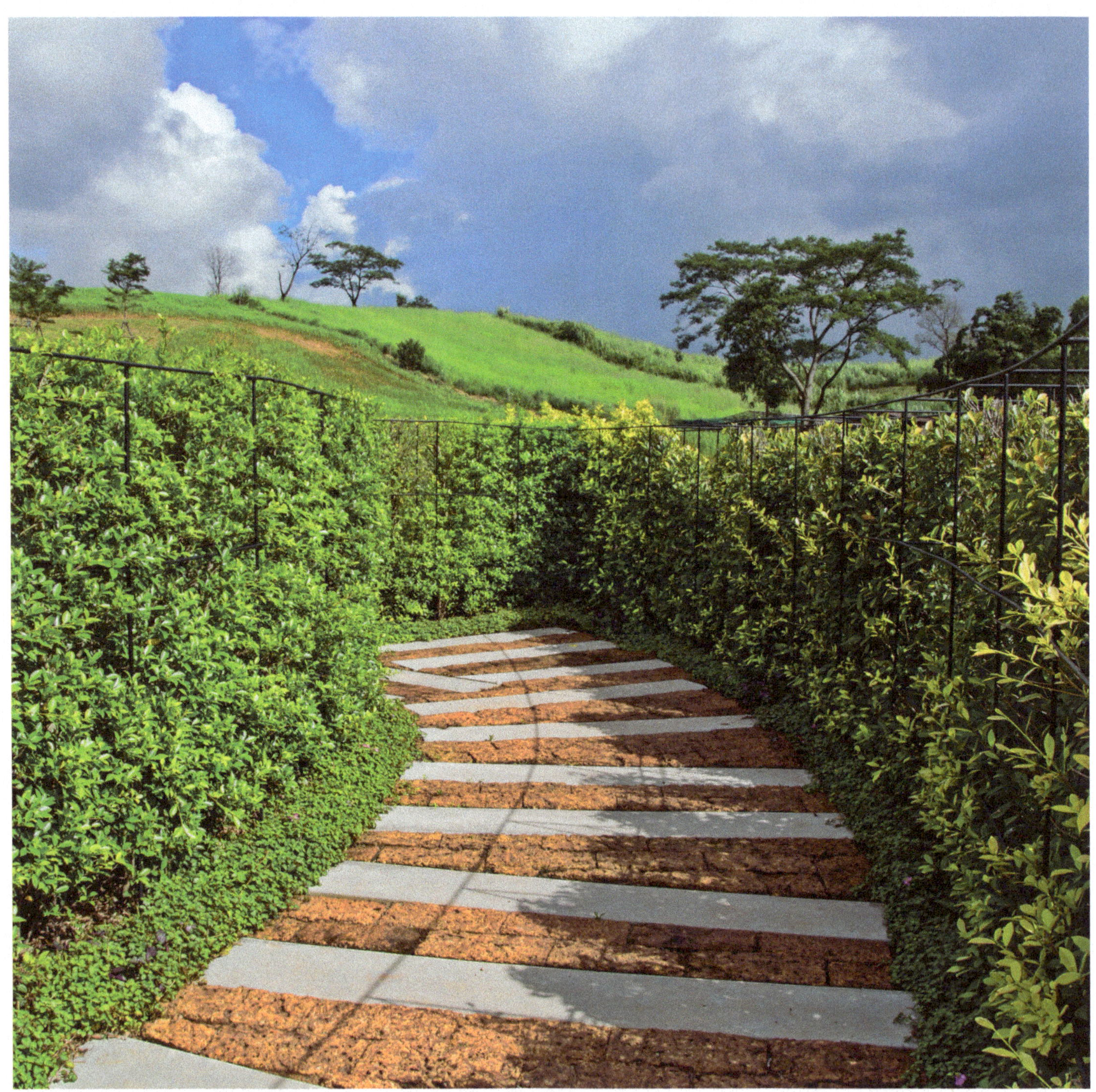

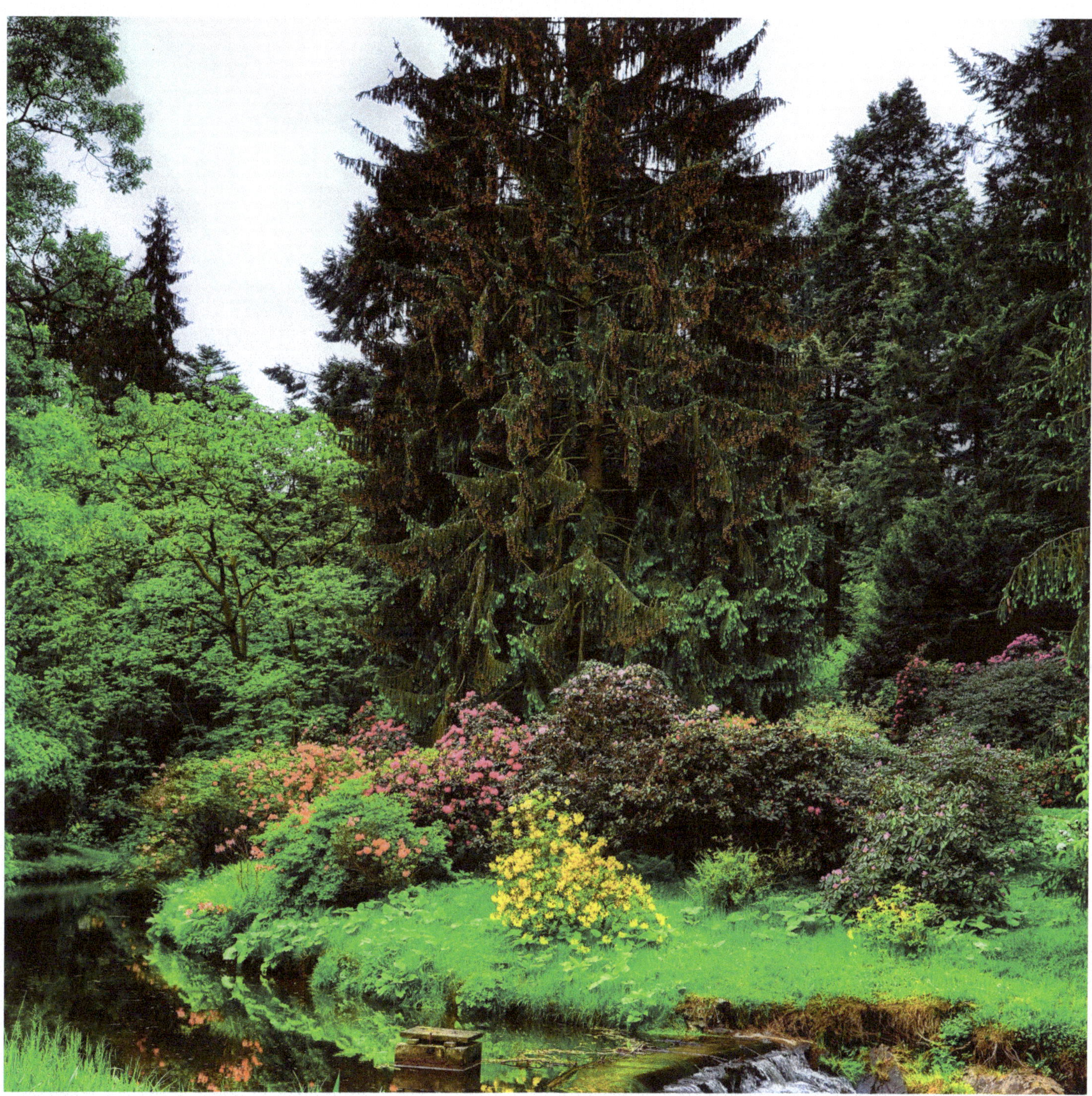

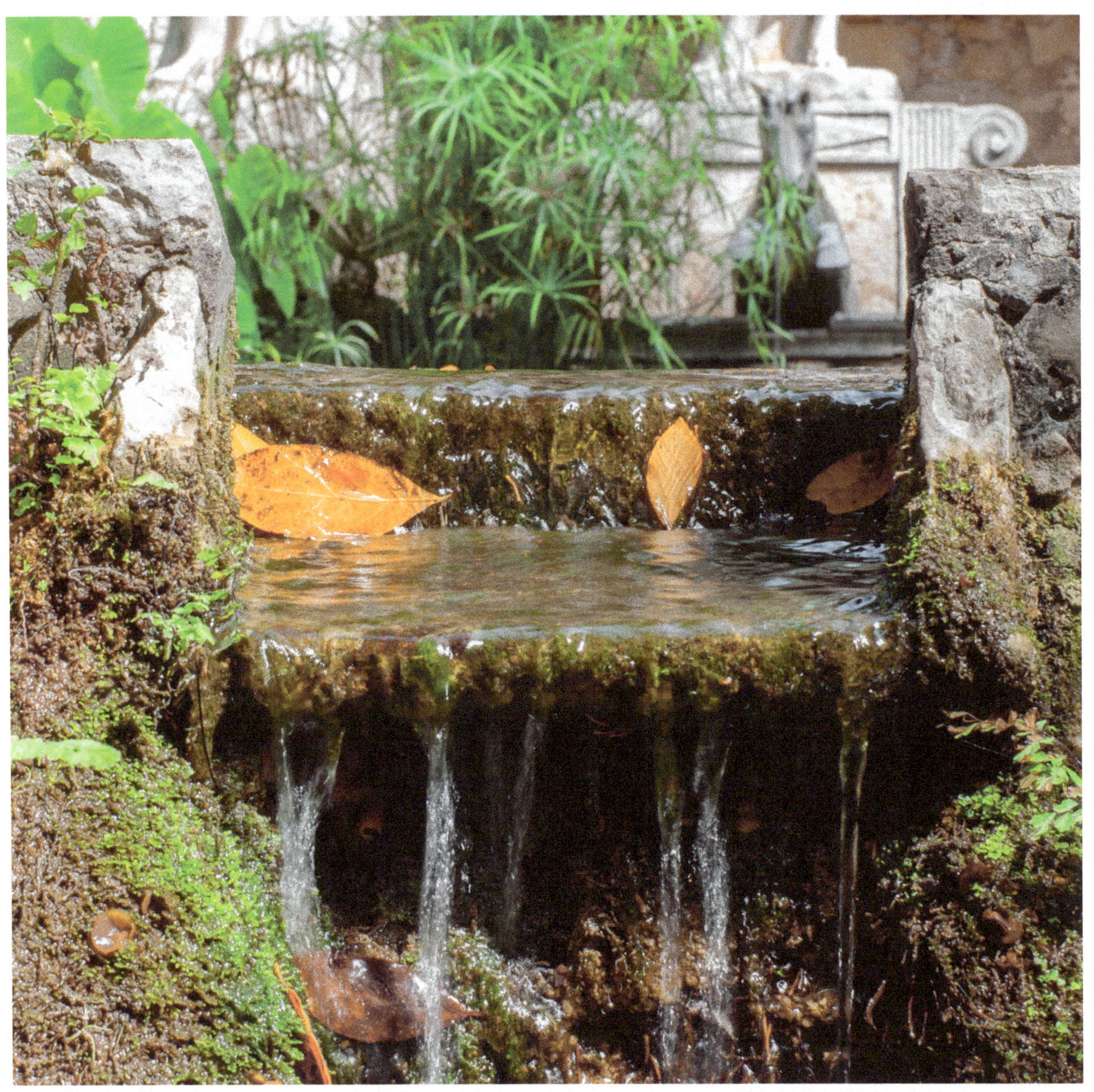

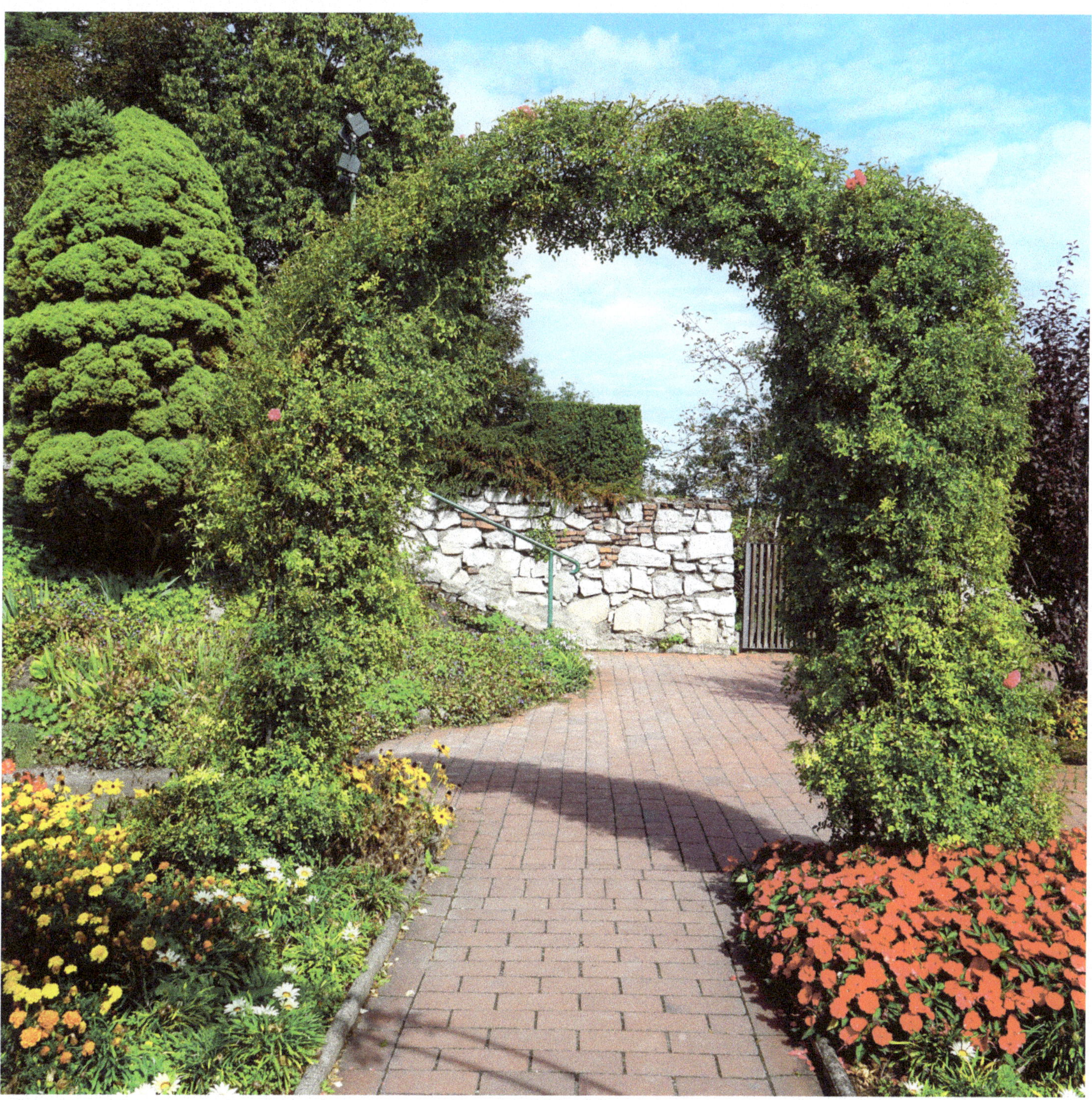

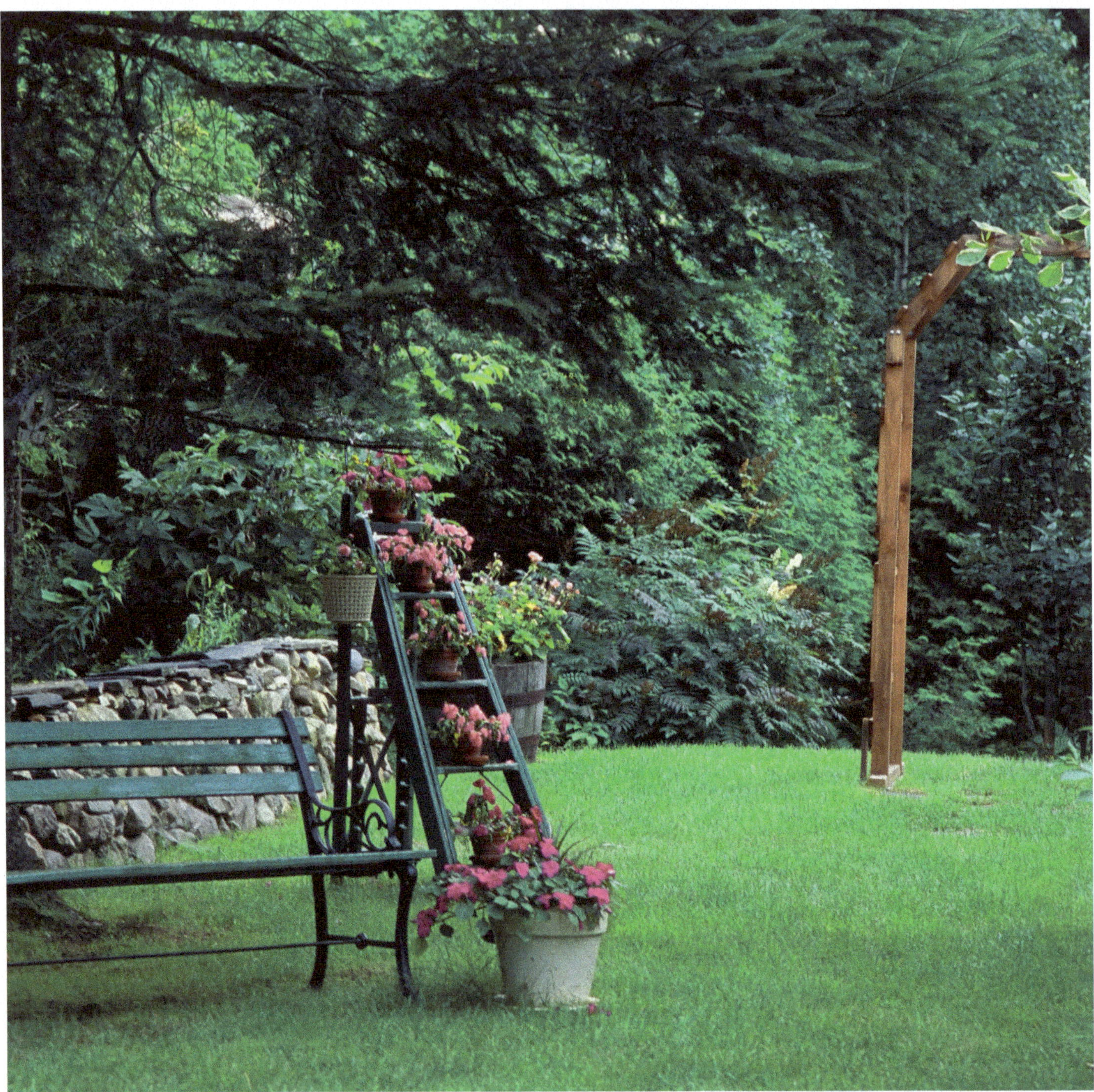

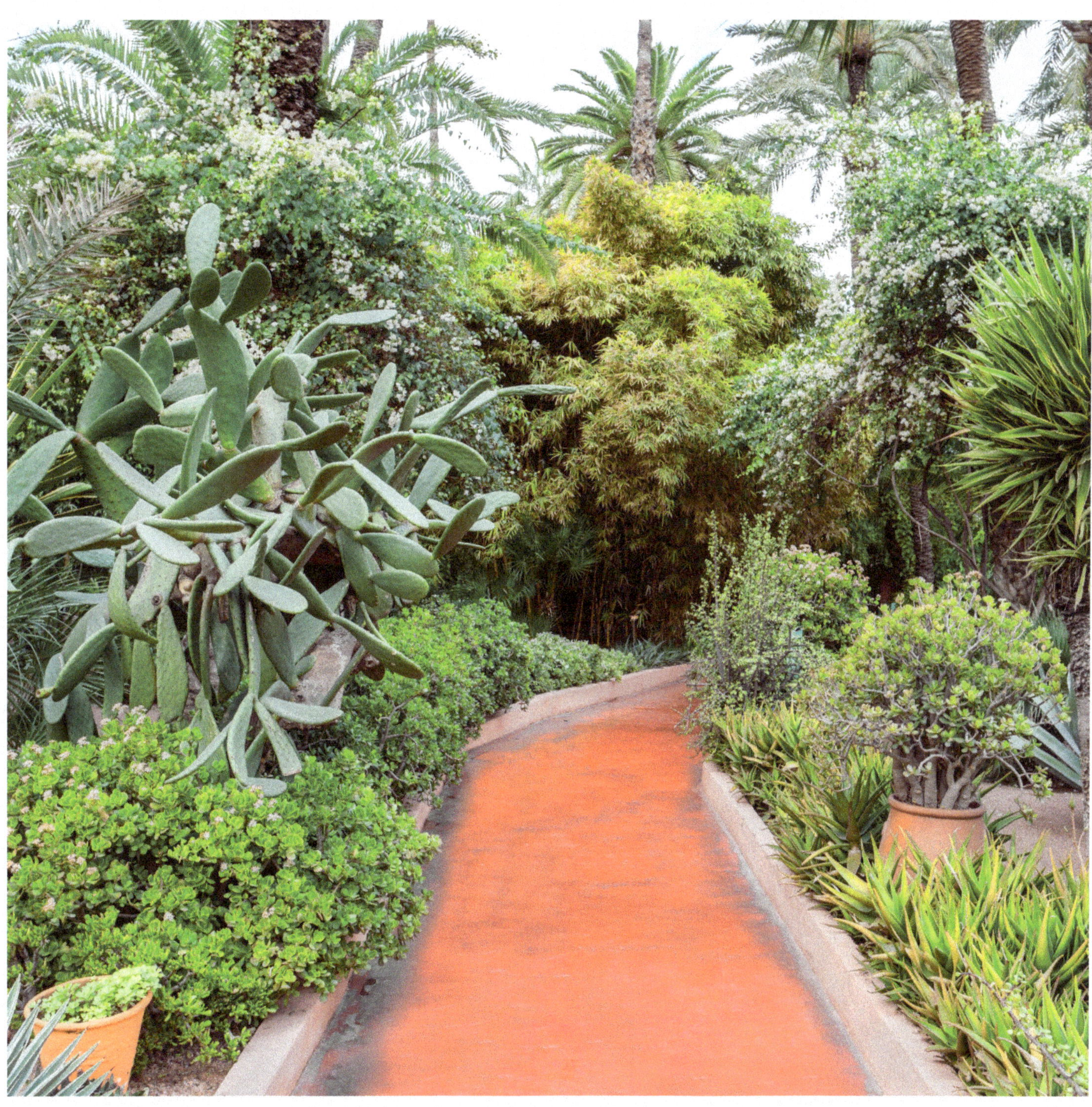

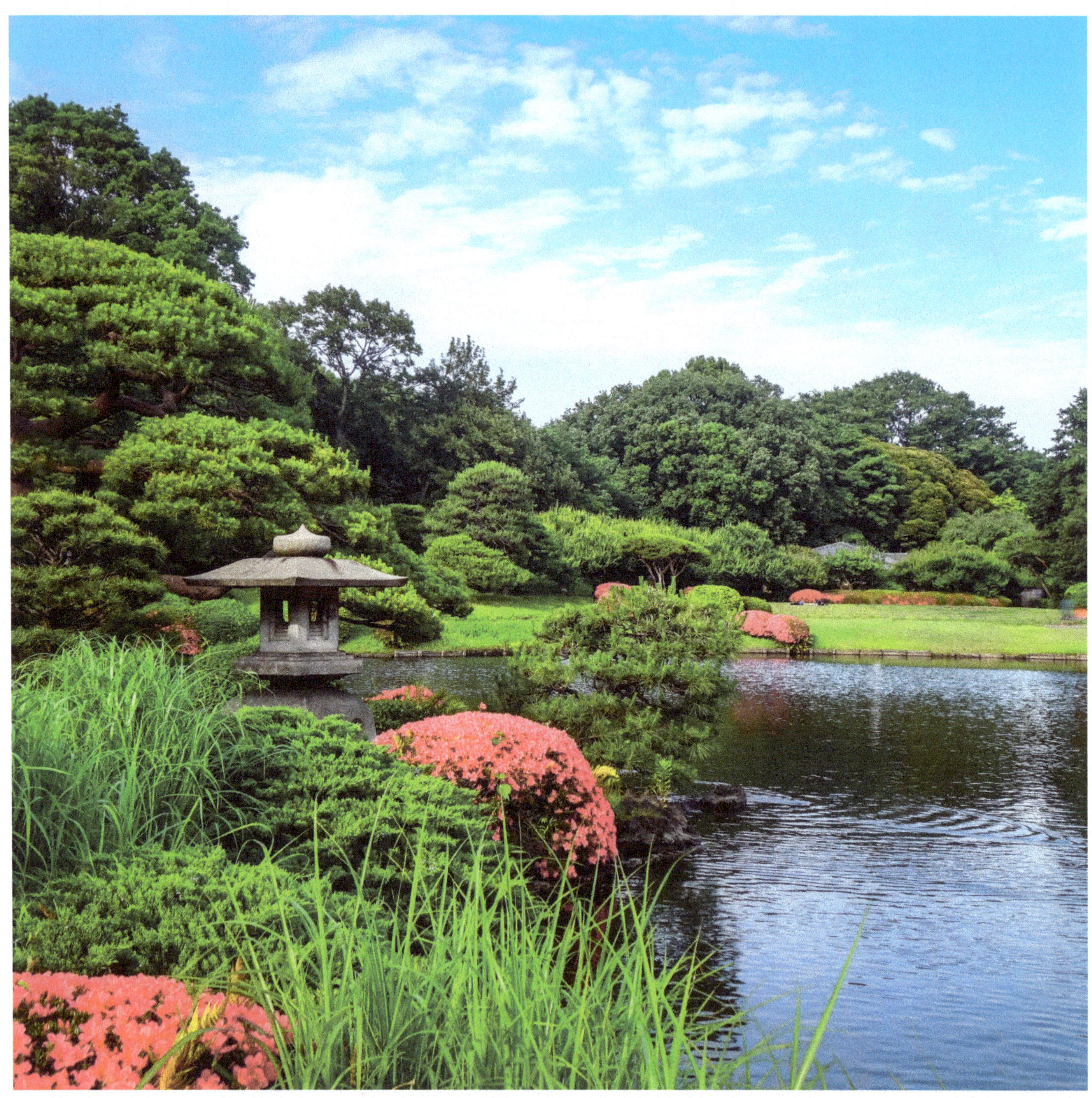

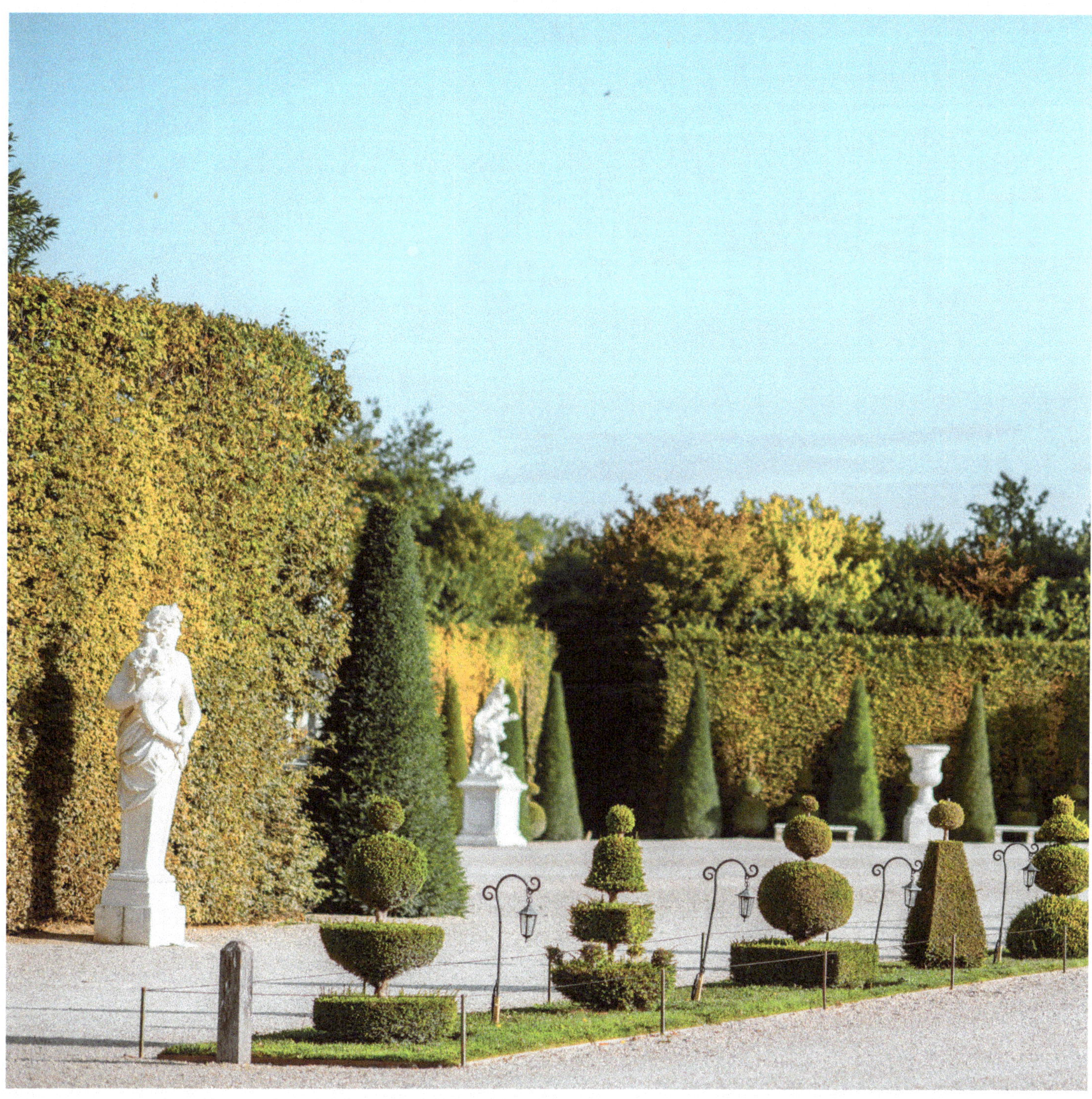

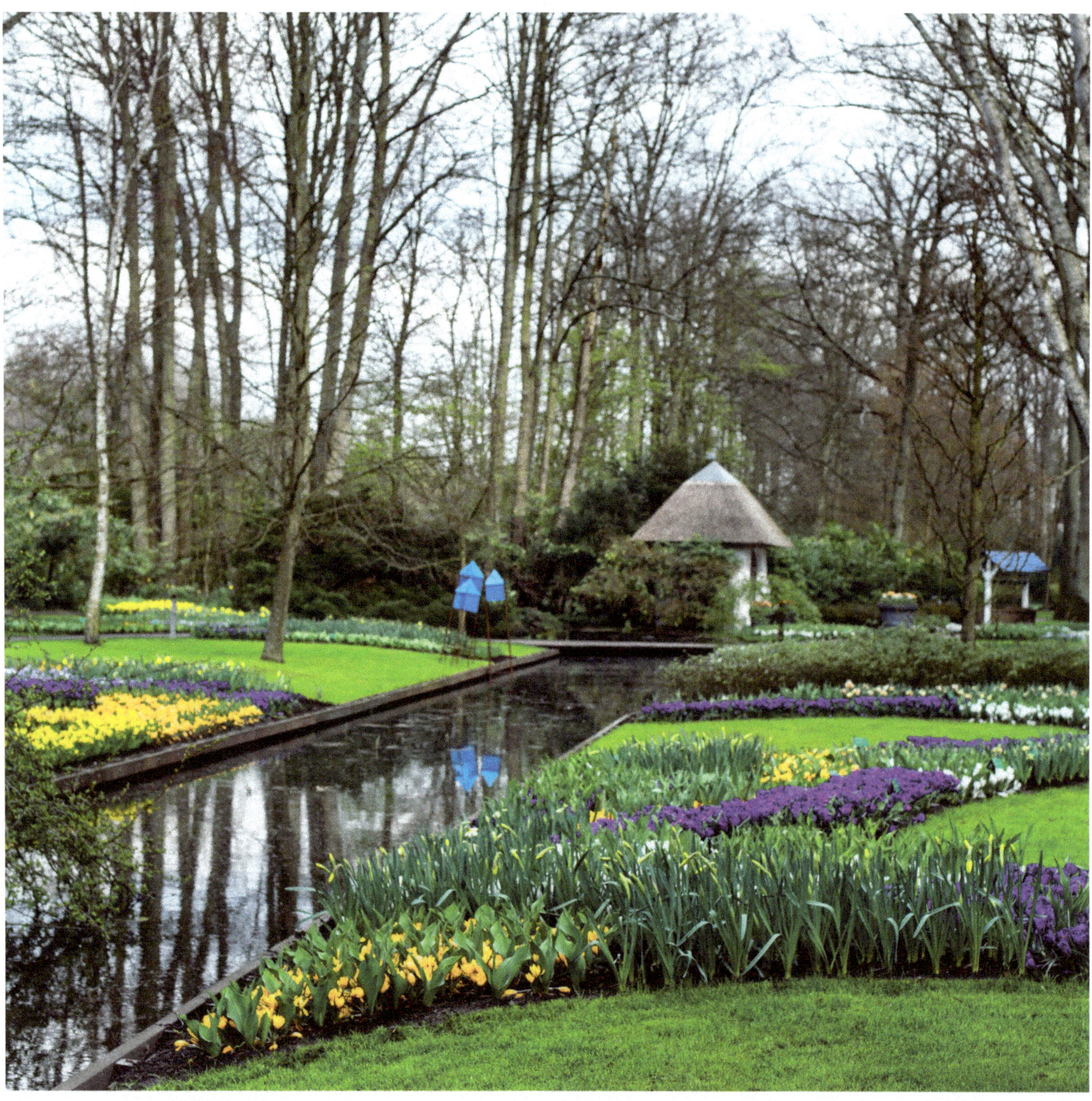

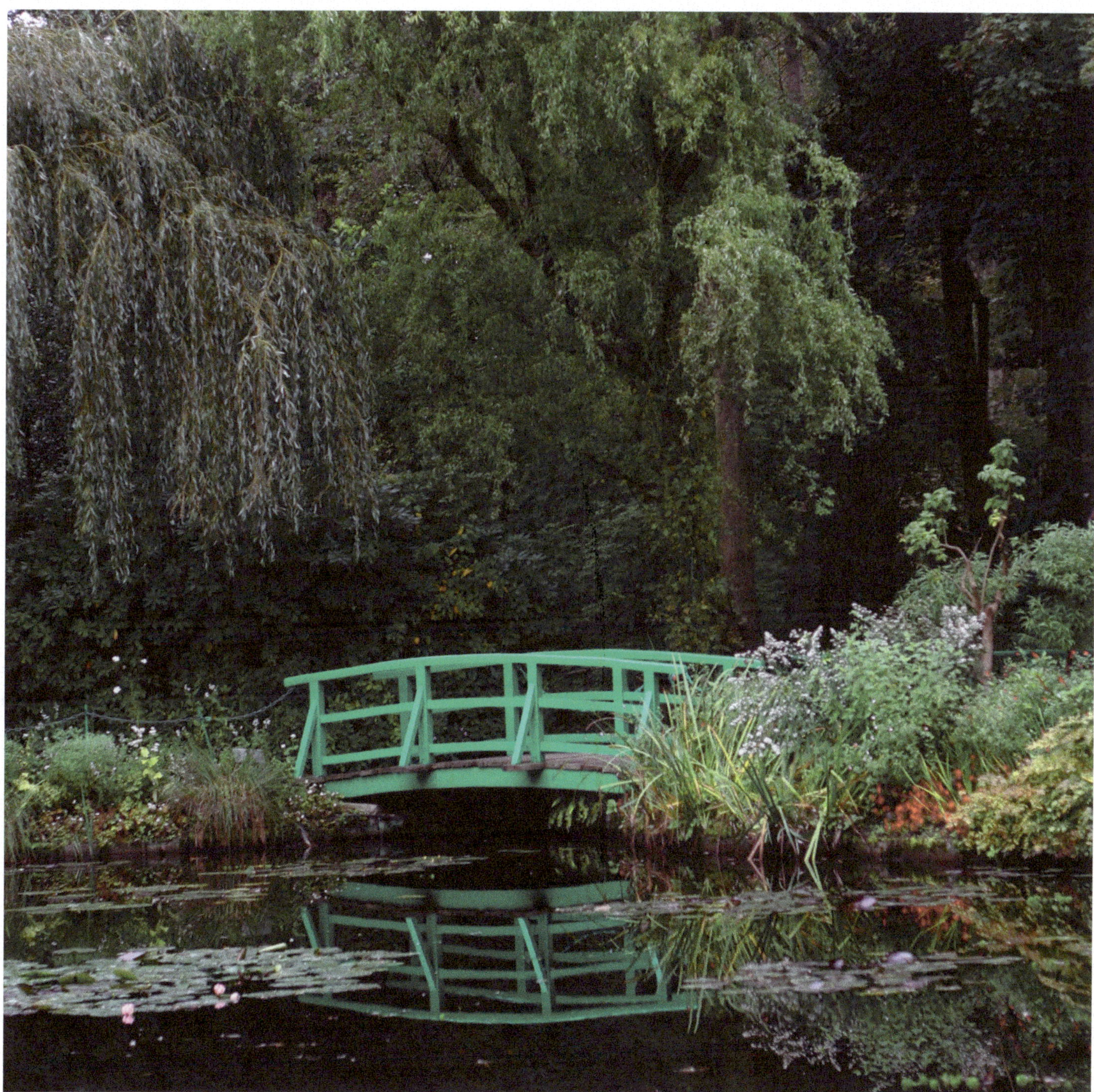

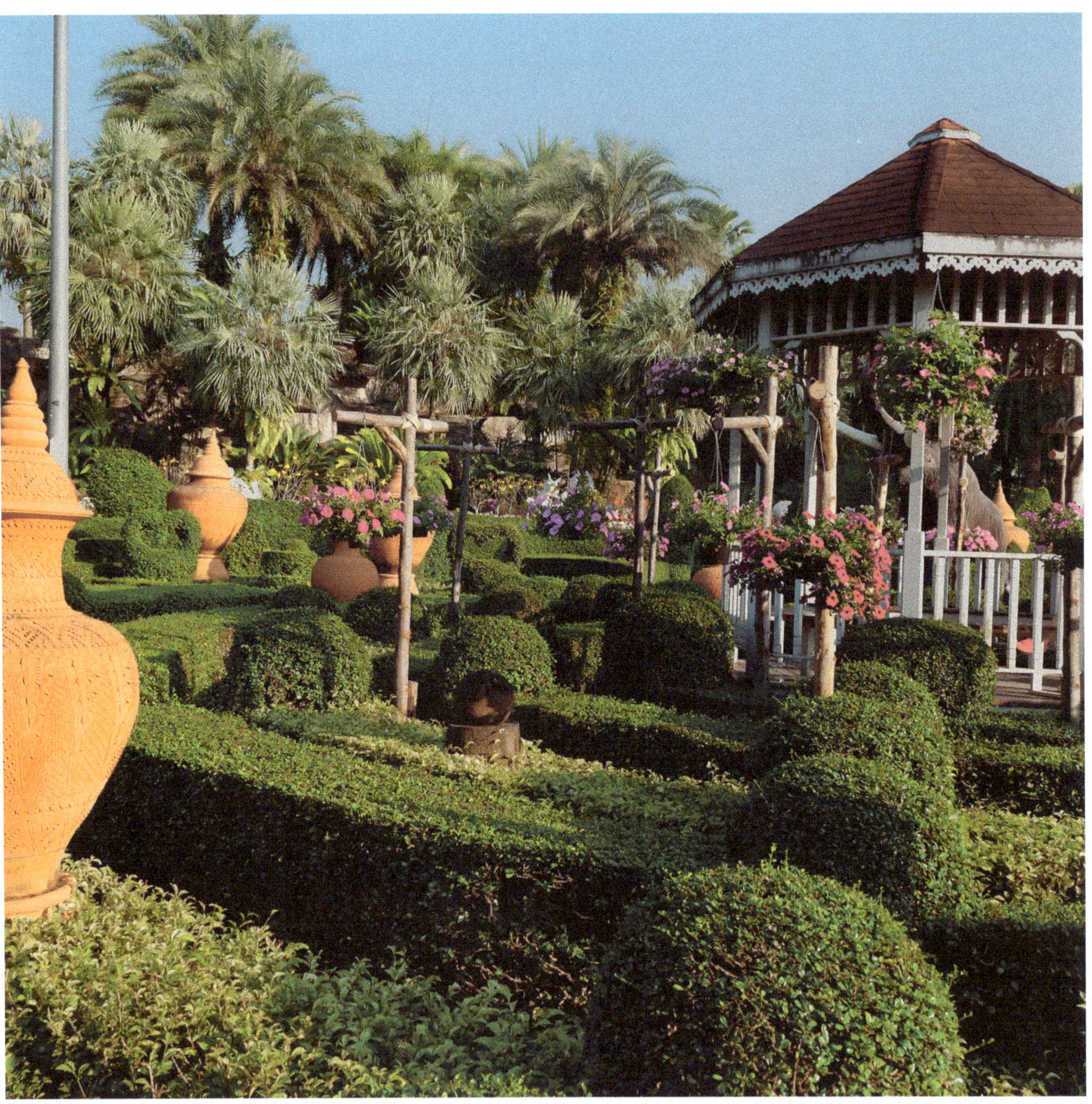

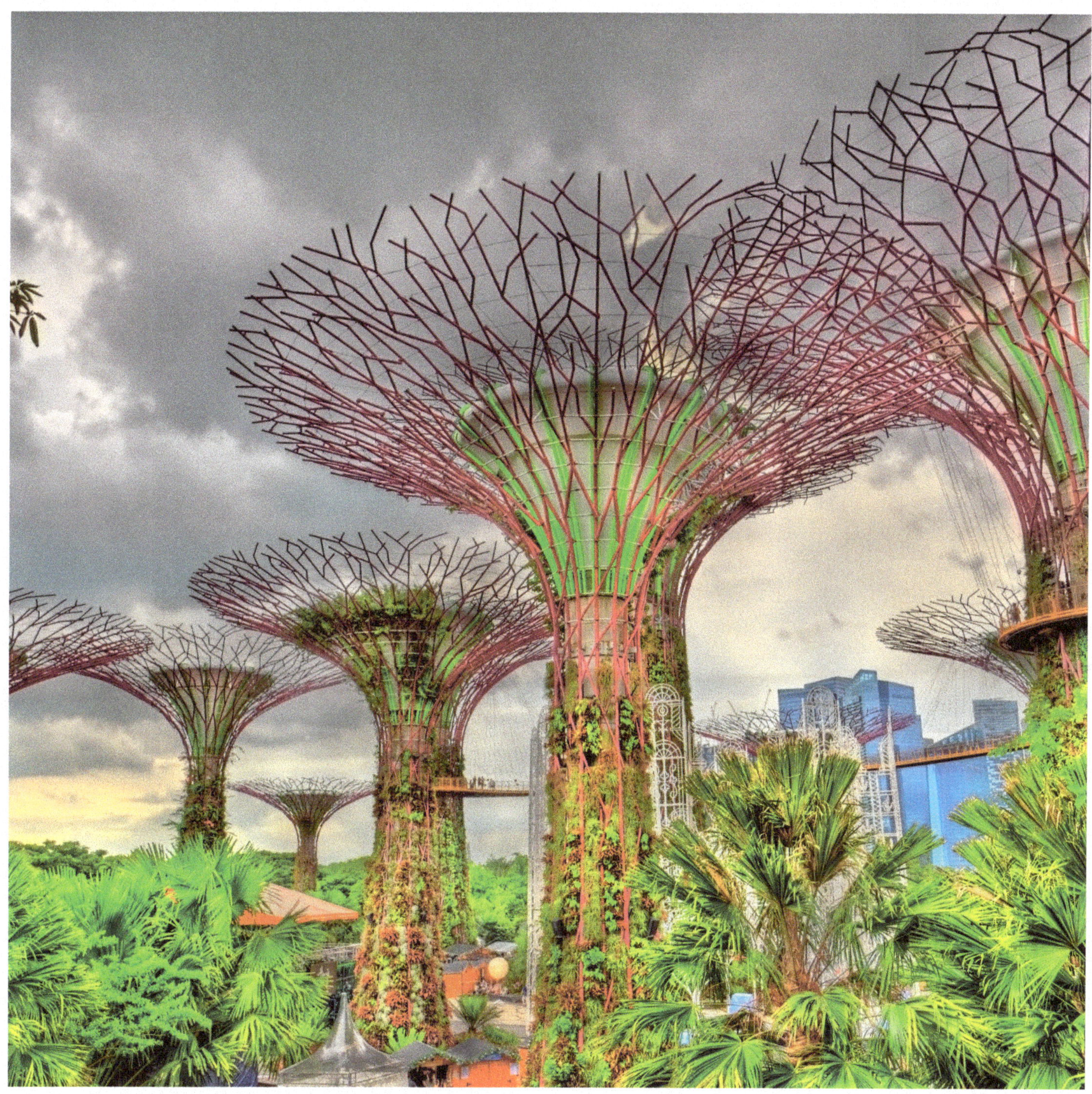

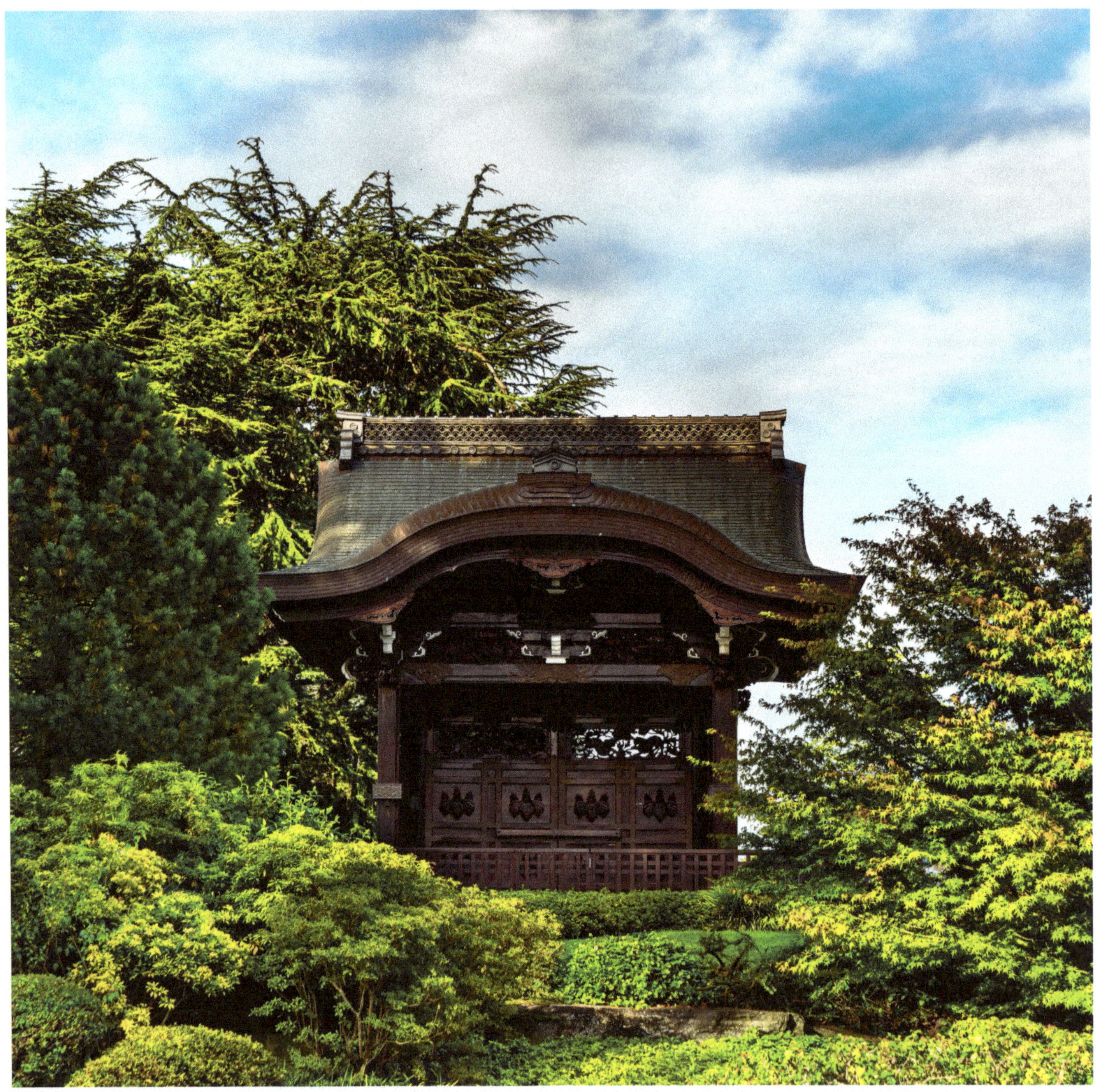

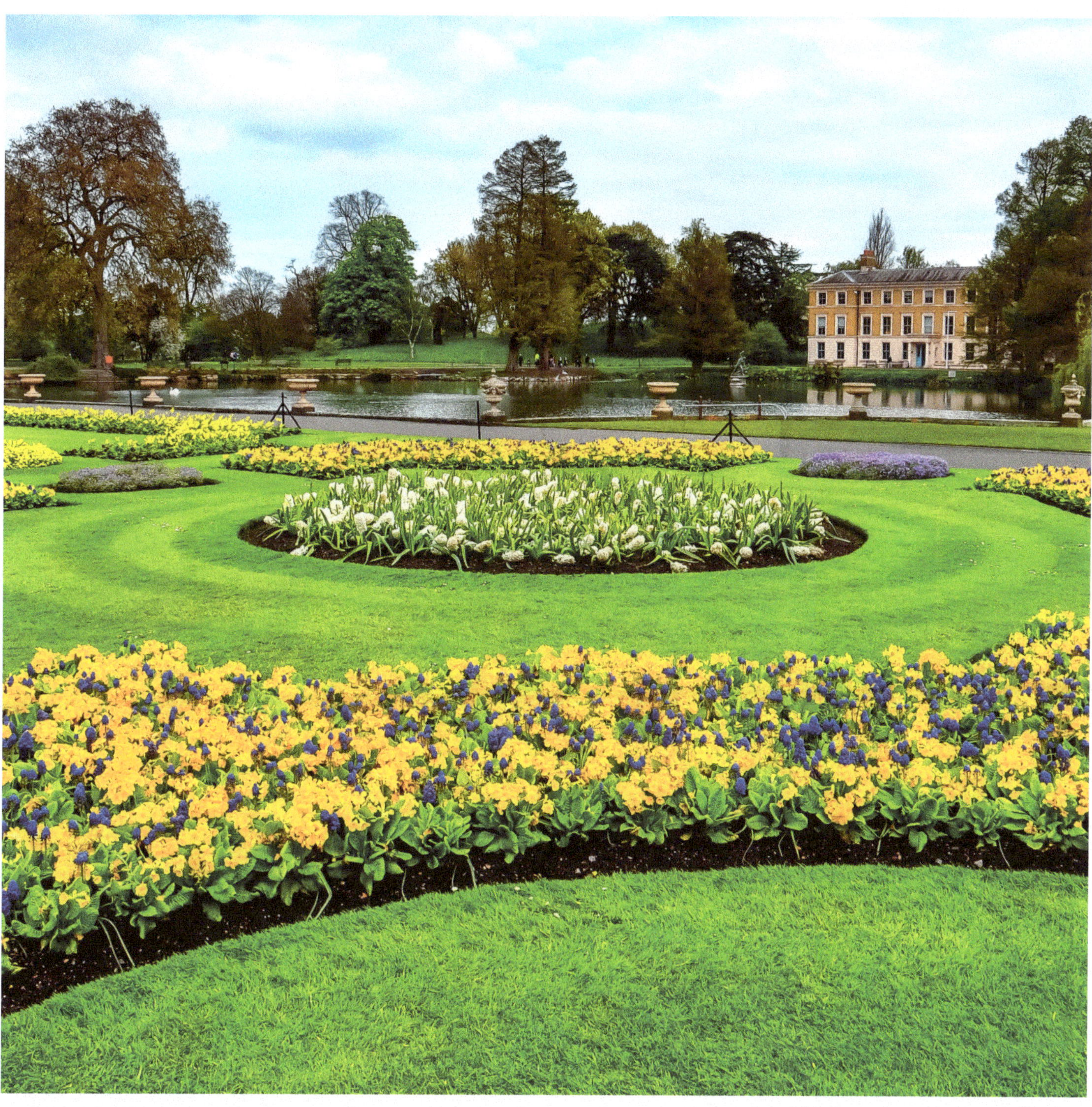